Hi Debs

May the stars of ... shine brightly on your path

[signature]

At David C Cook, we equip the local church around the corner and around the globe to make disciples. Come see how we are working together—go to **www.davidccook.org**. Thank you!

What people are saying about ...

THE UNKNOWN GOD

"How can the world religions be so drastically different and yet also uncannily similar and possibly related? Isn't it incomprehensible that the great faiths are both strikingly contrasting but also remarkably overlapping and even convergent? Might these paradoxical observations be resolved because Jesus is both the unavoidable stumbling block that sets Christianity apart but yet perhaps also the one way that somehow they all point to? *The Unknown God* invites readers on a journey to consider these questions in light of a gospel that challenges, even as it opens up conversation with, people in other faiths."

Dr. Amos Yong, Dean, School of
Theology and School of Intercultural
Studies, Fuller Theological Seminary

"Author Eugene Petersen observed that we have two mental operations that work in tandem—explanation and imagination. And hardly anything grips our imagination as a well-written story, inviting us to enter the story and play our part in the unfolding drama. What an exciting way to learn about an otherwise ho-hum topic—world religions. Read and enter."

Rev. Sunder Krishnan, Rexdale Alliance,
Toronto, Author: *The Conquest of Inner Space*

"God is bigger than our boxes! Firmly planted in Jesus' claims of exclusivity for salvation, Mathew discovers 'God's redemptive grace lurking in the dark and hidden corners of different religions.' *The Unknown God* will confirm and stretch your beliefs at the same time."

Dr. Craig Sider, President, New York City Leadership

"This book is a generous, thoughtful, nuanced, and compelling exploration of six faith traditions and their views of Jesus, written by a scholar who is himself a committed follower of Jesus. This is a book to share with your friends."

Dr. Richard Peace, Professor of Spiritual Formation, Fuller Theological Seminary, Author: *Noticing God*

"The book, birthed out of personal experience and passion, is an excellent resource for all of us to understand our neighbour's perspective and the gifts we all have to give one another. In a world where more compassion, respect, and understanding is so desperately needed, *The Unknown God* is a timely bridge in a sea of walls."

Christa Hesselink, Author: *Life's Great Dare: Risking It All for the Abundant Life*

"*The Unknown God* offers an incredible resource to people of all religious backgrounds, particularly Christians who are looking to understand world religions and how people can talk together in a respectful and thoughtful way about their beliefs. The author's breadth of knowledge, thoughtful insights, and conversational approach are a very rare combination and make it easy for people to grasp the beliefs of world religions, learn from each other, and also consider the life and message of Jesus in light of world religions. I highly recommend this book."

Tim Day, The City Movement,
Author: *God Enters Stage Left*

"The author dared to proclaim Christ as the way, the truth, and the life in a world culture that is not open to such claim ... He describes how other religions picture Christ and anybody—not just Israel—could have access to Father God, through Jesus Christ, and be His friends and children with all the promises and its benefits that come with faith in Christ, which is the only true way of Salvation."

Rev. Thomas Kutty, National Leader
(Emeritus), The Foursquare Church in India

"This book will lead you to your own personal encounters with Jesus, but in the process, will also help you discover the star that illuminates the path to that encounter!"

Dr. Johnny Ramirez-Johnson, Professor of
Anthropology, Fuller Theological Seminary

THE
UNKNOWN GOD

THE
UNKNOWN GOD

A JOURNEY WITH JESUS FROM EAST TO WEST

MATHEW P. JOHN

DAVID C COOK

transforming lives together

THE UNKNOWN GOD
Published by David C Cook
4050 Lee Vance Drive
Colorado Springs, CO 80918 U.S.A.

Integrity Music Limited, a Division of David C Cook
Brighton, East Sussex BN1 2RE, England

The graphic circle C logo is a registered trademark of David C Cook.

Details in some stories have been changed to protect
the identities of the persons involved.

Christian Bible credits are located at the back of the book. The author mostly relies
on his personal knowledge of ancient languages to translate the sacred scriptures of
different religions. Since there are variant texts and multiple translations available, the
quotes from the scriptures might appear similar to or different from any given source.

Library of Congress Control Number 2019948098
ISBN 978-0-8307-8074-7
eISBN 978-0-8307-8101-0

The Team: Michael Covington, Jeff Gerke, Stephanie Bennett,
Jon Middel, Megan Stengel, Susan Murdock
Cover Design: James Hershberger

Printed in the United States of America
Second Edition 2020

1 2 3 4 5 6 7 8 9 10

121619

To
Joanne
best friend,
fiercest critic,
and
one true love.

CONTENTS

FOREWORD

I entered first grade in 1954 when the US Congress added the phrase "under God" to the Pledge of Allegiance. Two years later, "In God We Trust" replaced "E pluribus unum" on the Great Seal of the United States and began appearing on the nation's currency. Americans took pride in being a religious people, and by "religious," they meant *Christian*.

In those days, finding a mosque or a Hindu temple in suburbia was about as likely as spotting a UFO. My, how things have changed in six decades. Now, Hollywood celebrities openly convert to Buddhism, two of Silicon Valley's tech giants are led by Hindus, and Muslim candidates run for national office.

Meanwhile, a growing minority is opting out of religion altogether. The number of Americans unaffiliated with any religion has quadrupled since 1991 and includes 38 percent of citizens between the ages of eighteen and twenty-nine. When polled, these unaffiliated, or "nones," often cite the narrowness and exclusiveness of Christian churches as barriers to faith.

Enter Mathew John, whose life seems scripted to offer guidance to a newly pluralistic society. Raised in a Christian home in a nation dominated by a billion Hindus, he attended school in a city known for its historic Jewish settlements. From there, he entered Mahatma Gandhi University, where he was assigned a devout Muslim roommate. Further studies in Toronto and greater Los Angeles exposed him to even more diversity.

With a master's in theological studies and a PhD in intercultural studies, Mathew is uniquely qualified as a guide. Moreover, he has the ability to break down the complexity of religions and make them understandable. He uses *The Simpsons* and *Avatar* to teach about Hinduism, and *Seinfeld* and *The Matrix* to give insights into Buddhism. He draws striking parallels from the Bible, for example, asking, "What if God were to ask a televangelist to go and preach repentance to the jihadists wreaking havoc in the Middle East? ... God once asked something very similar of a prophet named Jonah."

From his many encounters with other religions, Mathew personally grappled with the questions that challenge spiritual seekers. Why does the Bible place such emphasis on a tiny tribe of Israelites that became known as the Jews? And when one of those Jews announces, "I am the way, the truth, and the life. No one comes to the Father except through Me," where does that leave the billions of people who never heard of Jesus?

In Jesus, who changed history more than anyone who has ever lived, Mathew finds a commonality among the various religions. Hindus see Jesus as a godly incarnation, and Buddhists recognize Him as a fully enlightened one. Muslims recognize Jesus as a prophet second only to Muhammad, who will return in a Second Coming to set right the world; the Quran calls Him "the Messiah" and acknowledges His virgin birth to Mary, the only woman mentioned in the Quran.

Mathew explores "Christ figures" present in other religions that point to Jesus. Christians are familiar with many of these in the Old Testament, such as the Passover meal and the Suffering Servant of Isaiah, but less familiar with parallels in other religions. C. S. Lewis spoke of "true myths," or Christ archetypes, imprinted in other religions that actually point to Christ. The Bible itself shows God using an Egyptian king and pagan priests, as well as many ordinary Gentiles, as part of God's plan of self-revelation.

There was an era, in my own lifetime, when the US took for granted the Christian faith as a kind of national religion. That time has passed. Christianity has traveled far beyond its historic roots in Europe and the Americas and has spread, as Jesus predicted, to the uttermost parts of the earth. We face new challenges not only internationally but also within our own borders.

In his winsome style, Mathew offers an approach that stresses understanding and unity rather than division. Not everyone will agree with his conclusions. But we dare not shrink from the challenge he presents. I find this book to be a helpful model that the church badly needs, and an important reminder of "the wideness in God's mercy."

Philip Yancey

ACKNOWLEDGMENTS

The narrative of this book unfolds as a personal spiritual journey from the East to the West, which I embarked on years ago, both literally and figuratively. This journey took place in the company of many fellow pilgrims. You, my reader, are the last one I meet on this road; so let me start by thanking you for picking up this book.

The content of this book is drawn from a series of seminars on the Christian response to world religions that I have been offering at various academic and ecclesiastical platforms currently available as "The Mosaic Course."

I want to thank the board of directors and the ministry partners of Focus Infinity Intercultural Outreach Network, the not-for-profit organization behind The Mosaic Course, for their unwavering support and constant encouragement, without which an endeavor of this magnitude would have been impossible to undertake. I also want to thank the cowriters of The Mosaic Course: John Bowen, Joshua Thambiraj, Thomas Leung, Mona Scrivens, Maria Short, Muhammad (Sam) Nasser, and Dan Stephenson, for enriching the course with insights from different cultural and theological perspectives.

The project was initially conceived of as a series of booklets written by different authors, but I decided to go back to the original content of my seminars and write it out as a "story." In this process I have drawn from many personal encounters I have had with people of different religious backgrounds. Although I have used creative license to alter their names and the details of these episodes, I want to gratefully acknowledge the significant contribution they have made to the content of this book.

Coming straight out of a doctoral dissertation and an academic book project with a major publisher, I needed to reinvent my language, tone, and style for this book. My first editor, Keely Boeving, helped me do just that, and much more.

The draft was then discovered by Michael Covington, who championed the project at David C Cook and put together "my tribe"—which included Jack Campbell, Megan Stengel, Nathan Landry, Andrew Brown, James Hershberger, Rex Louth, Jeff Gerke, and Annette Brickbealer. It is this dream team that helped me reframe my arguments from the perspective of the prospective readers and find the right balance between academic and "popular" writing.

The true inspiration for this book came from a fortuitous invitation I received from my favorite author, Philip Yancey, and his gracious wife, Janet, to join them on a weeklong trip to India. I have since had the privilege to learn from the "Yancey I never knew"—an experience that has challenged me to approach a contentious topic like apologetics with an attitude of humility and grace. I am deeply indebted to their kindness and generosity, and grateful for their unmitigated support to my ministry.

I have dedicated this book to my wife, Joanne, who was providentially matched with me through a cosmic algorithm commonly called "arranged marriage." I want to thank her, not only for being my faithful partner for the last twenty-one years and counting (it merits a big round of applause in itself, if you know me at all), but also for her creative contributions reflected in every page of this book. I also thank our gracious children, Hannah and Emma, for tolerating a writer-dad, who keeps swinging back and forth from alternate realities, even during family meals. I promise to do better, and vow to dedicate my next book to you.

Mathew P. John

"Here I am, I have come—it is written about me in the scroll."

Psalm 40:7 (NIV)

PROLOGUE

My story begins on a cold December morning in a tiny village in southern India.

The celestial sound of the *Gayatri mantra* floats along the tender mist, waking up the world to a bright and blessed morning.

> *Om tat savitur varenyam*
> *Bhargo devasya dhîmahi*
> *Dhiyo yo nah prachodayât*

The age-old prayer of the sages fills the air with the profound presence of the sacred.

> Oh God! Creator of the universe,
> May we receive Thy supreme light,
> May Thou guide our intellect in the right direction.

The Gayatri mantra is known as the mother of all mantras in Hinduism. It is an integral part of temple rituals and a customary incantation at any auspicious occasion. This primeval chant has been the "morning alarm" for every Indian for generations.

The quest for *Savithur*, the Supreme Light, initiates the spiritual journey of a Hindu. During the initiation rites (*upanayana*), the priests recite the Gayatri mantra directly into the ears of their pupils. Once the initiates themselves perfect the chant, they are considered twice born (*dwijan*). They have stepped into a new realm of consciousness, and their spiritual journey is guided by the quest for the Supreme Light from now on.

As the soothing chants of the Gayatri mantra melt into my soul, a piercing voice explodes from a loudspeaker:

> In him was life; and the life was the light of men.
> And the light shineth in darkness;
> and the darkness comprehended it not.[1]

The reading comes from a church building across the street from the Hindu temple. The curate is reciting from the Bible in preparation for the commencement of the morning mass.

> That was the true Light, which lighteth
> every man that cometh into the world.[2]

I feel like I am in the middle of a conversation—a dialogue between two great world religions. The Scripture verses descending from the church dome seem to answer the Vedic prayer rising from the temple steeple. One searching for the Supreme Light that enlightens the universe; the other declaring its arrival into our dark and desolate world.

"I am the Light of the world," says Jesus Christ.[3]

Is the Christian Scripture responding to the prayers of the ancient sages?

Lying there, as a boy of twelve, I begin to wonder …

Chapter 1

FOLLOWING THE STAR

I permitted Myself to be sought by those who did not
ask for Me;
I permitted Myself to be found by those who did not
seek Me.
I said, "Here am I, here am I,"
To a nation which did not call on My name.
—*Isaiah 65:1*

Your eyes will see this and you will say, "The LORD
be magnified beyond the border of Israel!"
—*Malachi 1:5*

In the southern tip of India, there is a tiny state called Kerala.
Sandwiched between an ocean and a mountain, it features one of the
most scenic landscapes in the tropical region. The exquisite terrain of
Kerala once inspired *National Geographic* to run an exclusive feature
that described this land as "the Jewel of India's Malabar coast."[1]

Kerala is believed to be the point of entry for Christianity in India. According to tradition, Thomas, the disciple of Jesus Christ, arrived in Kerala in 53 CE and planted the seeds of Christianity in the country. A couple of centuries later, a group of Syrian traders discovered this remote Christian community and brought it under the folds of the Syrian Orthodox Church in Antioch.

I was born into one of these "Orthodox" families, which claimed its Christian heritage all the way back to the first century. But I did not want anything to do with the God of Christianity. I grew up thinking that He was a racist.

Can God be a racist?

I was taught in Sunday school that the Jews are the "chosen people" of God. "Out of all the peoples on the face of the earth, the LORD has chosen you to be his treasured possession," says God to the Jews.[2] This didn't make sense to me. What kind of a God would choose one nation over others and call them "My people"? What kind of a father would pick a favorite among his children?

God's preoccupation with the Jewish nation made me feel invisible and insignificant. How, I wondered, could God be so blatantly biased toward one particular ethnic group? If Jews are God's people, then who are Indians (or Asians, Africans, or Caucasians, for that matter) to God? Why didn't He choose any of us?

Don't get me wrong. India boasts one of the earliest settlements of the Jewish diaspora, and I have had the privilege to have many Jewish friends and neighbors.[3] They are a wonderful people, of course. But as a child growing up in India, I did not understand why their story filled every page of the Bible, as if nothing happened elsewhere in the world. Why are the Jews considered "special" in the eyes of God?

It was in the midst of this internal wrestling, when I was about fourteen, that something eye-opening happened at my school.

I studied at a rural school in India, which enrolled over a thousand students from middle-class families. Funded by the local government, our student body did not have the luxury of organizing any type of recreational events. So we often turned to roadshow runners and street performers to provide us with our periodic dose of entertainment.

One day, a traveling magician presented an impromptu show at our morning assembly. He started with token tricks, such as pulling out candies and balloons from an empty hat, and soon proceeded to a more formal routine.

In the middle of the act, the magician called for a volunteer from the audience. All of us looked at each other. No one dared to go. We had seen magicians tossing their assistants across the stage, cutting them in half, and even making them disappear. What if he tried one of those menacing tricks on us?

The magician called out again, this time warning that if no one volunteered, he was going to randomly pick an assistant from the audience.

We crouched lower behind the seats as his eyes scanned the audience, avoiding eye contact as much as we could. After a few seconds of nerve-racking silence, we heard his voice:

"You, the one in the blue shirt, come up."

I looked up with a sigh of relief. Thank God, I was wearing a white shirt.

I turned around, looking in the direction the magician was motioning. There he was, the boy in the blue shirt—the chosen one. He was a chubby little kid whom all the bullies loved to pick on. He usually sat in the back of the class, ate his lunch alone, and spent most of his recess hours in the bathroom. The audience began snickering the moment they saw who it was.

As the boy in the blue shirt climbed onto the stage, the magician began pouring some milk into a glass, filling it up to the brim. He set it on a table in the center of the stage and turned toward his new assistant. "You are going to drink this milk through the air."

The magician handed an empty straw to the boy, who held it between his quivering lips. "Drink up, my friend," commanded the magician, waving his wand over the glass of milk with an enchanting gesture.

The boy stood there, befuddled, for a long second. The glass was at least twenty-five feet away from him and he had only a six-inch straw. His predicament was becoming highly entertaining to all of us.

All he could do was suck in air through the straw, and that is what he did. Suddenly the magic began to be unveiled. To our surprise, the milk in the glass started disappearing as he sucked on the straw. The audience gasped in disbelief. Was he actually siphoning the milk through thin air?

The milk finally reached the bottom of the glass. Even though he hardly knew what had just happened, the chosen one stood there triumphantly with a victorious smile on his face.

This might have been the end of the story. But the real magic happened only after the magician left the school premises. That dorky, friendless kid in the blue shirt suddenly became a superstar in the school. How in the world could he have drunk milk from that glass unless he had acquired some mysterious power from the magician?

The school journal ran a cover story on his extraordinary adventure. Girls began chasing their new heartthrob in the hallways. An entourage now protected the celebrity from his unruly fans. Even the teachers began to regale each other with the legend of the boy in the blue shirt.

A hero was born.

As far as the magician was concerned, the boy in the blue shirt was an arbitrary choice. He was not chosen because he was special. But he became special because he was chosen.

o o o

The history of Israel begins like most movie trailers: "One man, on a journey, to a land unknown …"

God picks a man. His name is Abraham. God establishes a covenant with him: "And I will make you a great nation, and I will bless you, and make your name great; and so you shall be a blessing."[4] Today, Abraham is considered a father figure to three major religions in the world: Judaism, Christianity, and Islam—the members of which surpass half the world's population.

Why did God choose Abraham over anyone else? I have no idea. Why did the magician choose the boy in the blue shirt? I don't know that either. One thing I do know, however, is that the act of choosing had nothing much to do with the merits of the chosen one.

The Hebrew Scriptures do not always paint a particularly flattering picture of Abraham. There is an incident, for example, where Abraham and his nomadic tribe arrive in the land of Egypt. He fears that his beautiful wife, Sarah, will attract unnecessary attention from the lustful eyes of Pharaoh. If the king comes to know that she is married to him, his life will be in danger. So Abraham forces Sarah to pretend that she is his sister.[5]

Later, as the story unfolds, Pharaoh finds out that he is about to commit adultery by marrying Sarah. The conscience-stricken king cries out in distress: "What is this you have done to me? Why did you not tell me that she was your wife ... so that I took her for my wife?"[6] Who is morally superior in this story—the chosen one who tried to trade his wife or the pagan king who refused to take the bait?

It is the mystery of God's election. He does not pick anyone based on his or her qualifications. God's choosing is always an act of grace. God did not pick Abraham because he was special. But, like the boy in the blue shirt, Abraham became special because he was chosen.

We often have a problem with the idea of choosing because our rational mind is trained to think in a dualistic paradigm. We tend to look at the selection of something in conjunction with a "rejection" of everything else. But that is not necessarily true in this case. The arbitrary selection of one assistant does not imply the rejection of the rest of the audience. Both the volunteer and the audience are equally important to the magician. As a matter of fact, the non-chosen ones are the true beneficiaries of the act being performed by the chosen one.

In a sense, Abraham is the boy in the blue shirt. He was called to demonstrate God's "magical" power to the rest of the world. God's covenant with him, if you read it closely, came with a footnote: "In you *all the families of the earth* will be blessed."[7] In other words, *the Jews were chosen for the sake of the Gentiles* as well and were meant to be a channel of God's blessings to everyone in the world.

The Jews are born into the center stage of God's magic show as it unfolds in time and space. A Jew is, by default, God's lovely assistant, and is equipped to function as a channel of His grace to "all the families of the earth."

The status of the chosen one has to be special, however. Whatever happens to the assistant invariably affects the course of the magic act. So the magician has to make sure that the assistant is rendered whole and invincible throughout the act. To do so, he establishes a "covenant" with him—a binding promise between the magician and the chosen one that ensures the best possible performance of the magic act.

Here is the catch. If we think that being "chosen" is a privileged status that comes with a platinum credit card and special lounge access, we couldn't be further from the truth. In our morally compromised world, chosen ones tend to have privileged status, and they get away with all the mistakes they make. But the Jews are not called into a privilege; rather, they are assigned a responsibility. The responsibility comes with a certain set of privileges, of course, but only because they are necessary to accomplish the given mission.

The magician has to pay a heavy price even for the most inadvertent mistakes made on the stage. Therefore, the assistant has to be maintained flawless and exemplary. That is the burden of his calling. The audience, on the other hand, need not be perfect, and their imperfections remain unobserved.

The chosen one has to be perfected on a continual basis. This is perhaps why the Jews have become the most persecuted people in the world and Israel the most misunderstood nation in human history.

Now I say under my breath: "Thank You, God, for *not* choosing Indians."

Let the boy in the blue shirt take the limelight. I would much rather watch him from the comfort of my balcony seat. I don't complain because I know God is equally interested in me, and His magic act is being performed for my sake as much as it is for the sake of everyone else in the world.

○ ○ ○

I grew up in a small town in India called Piravom. The word Piravom comes from the root word *piravi*, which literally means *birth* or *nativity*. According to legend, Piravom is the hometown of one of the magi, or Wise Men, who visited Jesus at His birth. It has a majestic cathedral dedicated to the magi, aptly named "The Church of the Holy Kings."[8] Even today, Piravom maintains a thriving Christian community that traces its history all the way back to the time of the magi.

At the time of Jesus' birth, India was one of the few cultures that had mastered the art of interpreting the cosmic connection between the stars and human destiny. It is believed that the Persian magi initially studied under Hindu sages, whom they described as the "magi of India."[9] The *Encyclopedia Britannica* postulates that at least one of the magi who visited Christ was from India, and this theory is widely accepted in the Christian tradition.[10]

Whatever the case may be, one fact remains indisputable: the Wise Men of the East, the earliest religious figures to worship Jesus, did not belong to the so-called "Judeo-Christian tradition." They were outsiders. They came from far outside the realm of the covenant God had established with Israel, His chosen nation.

How was this possible? How did the knowledge of the most pivotal moment in human history, God's descent into the earthly realm, reach the Eastern world before it did the Promised Land? How did these Gentile diviners figure out the birth of the Messiah, which the Jewish scribes and priests have still not recognized?

It is an irony that the "exclusive" covenant God established with Israel was, in fact, "inclusive" at its very heart. Although it was addressed to Abraham, as we have already seen, the covenant was meant for "all the families of the earth." In other words, the selection of Israel does not imply God's exclusivity to a particular nation; it rather demonstrates a sweeping inclusivity of the whole wide world.

God's first covenant came to Noah, elegantly wrapped in a rainbow. This was an "everlasting covenant between God and *every living creature of all flesh that is on the earth.*"[11]

But the universal language of the covenant changed its tone and vocabulary by the time it reached Abraham. The Abrahamic covenant was addressed to a specific group of people at a specific time in history. Why, just a few short generations after the covenant with Noah, was God suddenly disinterested in the rest of the world? Why did He decide to work exclusively with a particular racial group?

We find the answer to this question in the book of Genesis. In an episode entitled "Babel," we see a cultural calamity of seismic proportion happening in the world. Not so long after Noah's descendants repopulate the earth following the great flood, the people decide to build a tower to protect themselves from future disasters. It triggers a de-globalization process of sorts, resulting in cultural chaos and emergence of unique languages.

God could not have communicated to this cacophonous culture by picking up a megaphone and yelling at the crowd. He had to choose a specific group and entrust them with His message, hoping they would communicate it to the rest of the world. For reasons best known to Him, this is the way God prefers to operate in the world even today.

In any case, God chose Abraham, the boy in the blue shirt, as the bearer of His message. And He sent him out as His ambassador to the world. The tone of the revelation now changed from universal to particular, but the intended recipient of the covenant remained the same—"all families of the earth."

Abraham's descendants soon deceived themselves, however, into thinking that they were God's personal favorites. They overlooked the fact that being chosen had brought them not into a privileged status but into a crucial responsibility. The assistant ignored the audience and began to indulge in his newfound stardom.

The prophets kept reminding Israel that their mission was to be "a light for the Gentiles" so that they could bring God's salvation "to the ends of the earth."[12] The sacred temple in Jerusalem, the epicenter of God's presence on earth, was not a Jewish temple, they declared; it was rather a "house of prayer for *all nations*."[13]

Jews are not the only "people of God" in the world; God addresses even the Egyptians, the archenemy of the Israelites, as "My people."[14] The God who delivered Israel from the oppression of Egypt also delivers Egypt from its "oppressors." The God who promised the Messiah for Israel also promises "a Savior and a Champion" for Egypt. He who brought Israel out of Egypt also brings "Arameans from Kir" and "Philistines from Caphtor."[15]

The Israelites, however, didn't want to hear about the inclusive nature of God's message. Egyptians, Arameans, and Philistines were all hard-nosed enemies of Israel, sworn to wipe out the chosen people from planet earth. Egyptians enslaved Israel for nearly four centuries, and Arameans fought the kings of Israel sporadically. Remember the iconic evil giant, Goliath? He was a Philistine. How could the God of Israel act as an agent of salvation for these savage nations?

As one theologian puts it, Israel "largely forgot the fact that they were meant to be a missionary nation and their calling was meant to be translated into dynamic outreach."[16] So God scattered them among the nations. The Jews became a nomadic people wandering all over the world, moving from one tent to the next. God remained faithful, however, dispensing His grace and glory through them wherever they went.

When the assistant (Israel) walked off the stage and wandered among the audience, the Magician walked with him. As a result, everyone got to see the magic, up close and personal. In a strange and mysterious way, the Magician used even the apparent flaw in His assistant's character as an opportunity to demonstrate His dedication and commitment to the audience. The flickering flames of the "light of salvation" suddenly illumined the whole auditorium.

The Bible is the story of God's magic act in the world, but it is written from the perspective of Israel. It is a view of the stage given to us through the eyes of His assistant. It is the best narrative we can have and the only one we need.

But that does not mean we have the whole picture. There are numerous eyes staring at the stage, and they all have their own stories of the magic to tell. In the end, the magic transcends all narratives. God goes beyond all stories.

○ ○ ○

What if God were to ask a televangelist to go and preach repentance to the jihadists wreaking havoc in the Middle East? I wonder if he would go.

And yet God once asked something very similar of a prophet named Jonah. In fact, the poor preacher was forced against his will to go and preach to the Assyrian city of Nineveh.

"Should I not have compassion on Nineveh?" God asks Jonah.[17] Jonah does not respond, but the answer in his mind would have been a resounding "*No.*"

First, the Assyrians didn't worship the God of Israel. So why, Jonah might have wondered, should He be interested in their miserable lives? Second, they were a notoriously wicked nation that, by the standards of earthly justice, deserved neither mercy nor compassion. Third, they were the same people who would march into the Promised Land just a few decades later and obliterate the kingdom of Israel from the face of the earth.[18] Why would God want to save them?

And yet Jonah does, eventually, do what the Lord asked him to do. He goes to Nineveh and delivers the message, ultimately leading the Assyrians to repent from their evil ways. This is only one of the many instances in the Hebrew scriptures where God intervenes on behalf of people who are outside the chosen nation of Israel.

In the Chronicles of the kings of Israel, we meet the Egyptian king Neco leading a campaign against the Chaldeans. Josiah, the king of Judah, comes against him at Megiddo. But Neco does not want to wage war against Judah. "What have we to do with each other, O King of Judah?" asks Neco. "I am not coming against you today but against the house with which I am at war, and God has ordered me to hurry. Stop for your own sake from interfering with God who is with me, so that He will not destroy you."[19]

It is important to remember that Josiah was one of the very few righteous kings of Judah. Unlike most of his ancestors, he zealously followed the law of God. While Josiah reigned, God's favor was upon Judah and its king. So what authority does Neco possess by which he can claim to be God's spokesperson to Josiah? If God wants to speak to the king of Judah, He should rather send a legitimate prophet from His fold, not an alien king who worships the idols of Isis and Osiris.

Naturally, Josiah discredits the counsel of Neco and marches against Egypt. This decision happens to cost him not only his kingdom but also his life. In the surprising climax of the story, we realize that the Egyptian king was, in fact, speaking on behalf of the God of Israel. This is how the narrator describes the event: "nor did he listen to the words of Neco *from the mouth of God.*"[20] The words that came out of the mouth of the pagan king, we are told, actually were the very words of God.

In another instance, Abraham comes across a pagan priest named Melchizedek.[21] He greets Abraham in the name of his god, El Elyon.[22] Abraham does not insist that he should be greeted in the name of the "real" God, Yahweh. Instead, he gives his tithe, God's portion of his wealth, to Melchizedek. Later in the Scriptures, David prophesies that the Jewish Messiah would come as a priest in the line of Melchizedek, not in the line of traditional Levitical priesthood.[23]

Is the God of Abraham the same as the god of Melchizedek? Could it be that Yahweh and El Elyon are two different names of the same God? We will consider many such questions over the course of our journey through different religions in the world.

In the pages of the Bible, we meet many Gentile characters who seem to play active roles in God's redemptive plan for the world. Jethro, Moses's father-in-law, was once a priest to the pagan deities of Midian. But he acted as chief counsel to Moses in the Exodus mission.[24] Rahab, a prostitute, and Ruth, a Moabite, were women born miles outside the sphere of God's covenant. Yet they became pivotal figures in the history of Israel, finding their way into the genealogy of the ultimate Jewish hero, King David (and of Jesus Christ).

The Queen of Sheba was commended by Jesus Himself for her eagerness to learn from the wisdom of Solomon. King Hiram of Tyre, a pagan king, partnered with Solomon in building the first temple of Jerusalem.[25] King Cyrus of Persia, another Gentile ruler, received a divine appointment to build the second Jewish temple and was even called God's "anointed."[26]

It seems to me that God has been actively involved in the history of many nations outside the geographical borders of Israel. His reach includes the whole world. He is certainly interested in all of us.

Salvation may have been "from" the Jews, but it is not exclusively "for" the Jews.

o o o

In the gospels according to Mark and Luke, we find an encounter between Jesus' disciples and a young man who performs miracles in His name.[27] Impressed by his devotion and dedication, the disciples offer him an invitation to join their team.

Being part of the disciples' band meant working closely with Jesus. It would have been a dream come true for an aspiring minister. But the man declines their invitation. A Christ-follower who refuses an invitation to literally follow Christ? How could someone refuse to follow Jesus and still perform miracles in His name?

The disciples report the incident to Jesus, saying, "We tried to prevent him because he was not following us." After all, someone needs to safeguard the community against unaccredited preachers and their heretical teachings.

Jesus' response, however, is sobering: "Do not hinder him," says Jesus. "For he who is not against us is for us."[28]

In another instance, Jesus said that He had "other sheep, which are not of this fold."[29] Is this young man one of those sheep from the other fold? What, I find myself wondering, is this mysterious other fold?

Could there be a group of sheep that has never met the shepherd yet belongs to Him anyway?

I can offer various conjectures, but in the end, no one has any convincing answers to these questions. I have learned one thing from this story, however: God's providential grace in the world cannot be confined to the boundaries of a specific community. As passionate as I am about my church and the purity of its doctrines, who am I to say that whoever does not follow Christ with me does not follow Him at all?

It is true that God's offer of salvation is in one sense "exclusive"—it is not revealed to all religions and all cultures. But it is also "inclusive" in the sense that it originates in one community and flows into others. Few are chosen, so that many may receive.

The universal reach of the New Covenant was first revealed to the church when God asked Peter to visit a man named Cornelius.[30] This man was not a Christian, yet he was a "devout man" who "feared God with all his household" and "prayed to God continually."

It comes as a big surprise to Peter to know that God is interested in the prayers of those who are neither Jews nor Christians. He gets a rude awakening through a dramatic vision, in which God commands, "What God has cleansed, no longer consider unholy." This incident was likely foremost on Peter's mind as he wrote in his epistle that God does not wish "for any to perish but for all to come to repentance."[31]

To be elected in Jesus Christ means to be incorporated into God's mission of establishing His kingdom on earth. The kingdom of God is meant for all people. "There is no distinction between Jew and Greek," says Paul. "For 'whoever will call upon the name of the LORD will be saved.'"[32]

This "inclusive exclusivity" of the gospel is further amplified in Paul's letters, which reiterate the fact that God is "the Savior of *all* men."[33] He desires that "*all* people everywhere should repent,"[34] and for "*all* men to be saved and to come to the knowledge of the truth."[35]

As a Christian, I believe that the ultimate revelation of God comes to humanity in the person of Jesus Christ. I am now entrusted with the task of taking it to the four corners of the world. Like Israel became "a light to the Gentiles,"[36] Christians are appointed to be "the light of the world."[37] Today, many Christians have fallen into the same trap that snared the children of Abraham. We also delude ourselves, at times, into thinking that those who are outside the realm of this covenant do not matter to God at all. Let us not forget the fact that salvation is a call to responsibility, not to privilege. We are chosen not for our own sake, but for the sake of others.

o o o

"In Him we live and move and have our being."[38]

This is one of the most beautiful verses in the Bible. I often hear it quoted in liturgies, benedictions, and worship songs. I see it printed on bumper stickers and painted on church buildings. In a silent yet eloquent voice, this verse reminds us of the invisible presence of God in our everyday life.

Did you know that this verse actually comes not from the mouth of God, but from a pagan source? It is an excerpt from *Cretica*, a poem written by the Greek philosopher Epimenides, in the seventh century BCE.[39] Here is the full version:

> They fashioned a tomb for you, holy and high one,
> Cretans, always liars, evil beasts, idle bellies.
> But you are not dead: you live and abide forever,
> For in you we live and move and have our being.[40]

The writer of this poem, when he wrote about the "holy and high" god in whom "we live and move and have our being," was not thinking about the Christian God. He was, in fact, referring to the Greek god Zeus.

I wonder why Paul decided to incorporate the voice of a pagan poet into his Holy Spirit–inspired sermon. Further, why would Luke, the writer of the Acts, record it in a book that we revere as the Word of God? How could a pagan prophecy find its way into the sacred Scriptures of Christianity?

Let us rewind to the beginning of the story. The episode starts with Paul exploring the city of Athens as he waits for his colleagues at Mars Hill.[41] The idols in the city provoke his spirit. But instead of condemning the idolatry, Paul goes on to do a "show and tell" sermon, using one of their own idols for an object lesson.

The god at the center of Paul's message is "*Agnostos Theos*," or "the unknown god." The legend behind the unknown god was not unknown to the Greeks.[42] It had its origins in a plague that spread through Greece at the time of Epimenides, which created a nation-wide pandemonium. People offered sacrifices to appease the angry gods, as usual, but the plague continued to spread. There must be yet another god who was still not pleased, they thought, but no one knew who he was. So they built new altars in the name of an "unknown" god and offered blood sacrifices. As the story goes, the epidemic came to an immediate stop, and a new god found his way into the already crowded Greek pantheon.

"What you worship in ignorance, this I proclaim to you," says Paul to the Athenians, pointing to the altar of the unknown god.[43] He is not preaching a new god; instead, he is revealing the "hidden" God embedded in their own sacred stories.

The unknown god of the Athenians, all of a sudden, becomes a signpost that points to the God of the Bible.

The Mars Hill sermon, of course, is not a proof for Paul's endorsement of idol worship, nor does it show his indulgence in syncretic missional practices. It is, however, an affirmation of God's ubiquitous presence in every religion and in every culture.

This truth hit home when I started reading the Rig Veda, the four-thousand-year-old Hindu sacred text. One of the hymns of this ancient scripture is titled, believe it or not, "To the Unknown God."

To the Unknown God
(Mandala X Hymn 121 Rig Veda)
In the beginning there arose the Golden Child
As soon as born, he alone was the lord of all that is.
He established the earth and this heaven:
Who is the God to whom we shall offer sacrifice?
He who gives breath, he who gives strength,
Whose command all the bright gods revere,
Whose shadow is immortality, whose shadow is death,

Who is the God to whom we shall offer sacrifice?
He who through his might became the sole king
Of the breathing and twinkling world,
Who governs all this, man and beast
Who is the God to whom we shall offer sacrifice?[44]

Who is this "unknown god" to whom the Hindu *rishis* were offering sacrifices? Did the Agnestos Theos of the Athenians present himself in other religions and cultures as well?

Now I am beginning to understand how the Wise Men of the East discovered the trail of redemptive grace that led them all the way from the lingering shadows of darkness to the ultimate "Golden Child" who established the heavens and the earth. If the God of Israel revealed Himself outside the geographical borders of His covenant, it only makes sense that the "good news" of the arrival of His Son would spill outside the traditional boundaries of the church and stream into the hearkening ears of genuine seekers everywhere, including my ancestors.

In the following chapters, we will embark on a spiritual journey in the footsteps of the Wise Men, all the way from the East to the West. In this pilgrimage through six major religions in the world, we will encounter the silhouettes of the unknown god emerging from the deep recesses of their sacred scriptures. We will discover a resonating chord beneath the surface-level dissonance in their theology—a scarlet thread of redemption woven into the spiritual fabric of different cultures and religions across the world.

As we go through the belief systems and worldview assumptions of each tradition, watch for the traces of "hidden revelations" embedded deep within their religious consciousness. Jesus might appear incognito as an unknown god—an *avatar* in Hinduism, a *bodhisattva* in Buddhism, the living *shabad* in Sikhism, a prophet in Islam, and the Messiah in Judaism. Let the Star of the Savior shine brightly in your path and lead you from the unknown god of other religions to the revealed God of the Bible.

I am not one of the Wise Men, of course, but I am here to accompany you on the same trail traversed by them. All I can promise you on this journey is some stories for the road. I hope they will help you discover the vignettes of truth God has secretly implanted in world religions to prepare us all for His grand entrance into our world in the person of Jesus Christ.

Chapter 2

THE DESCENT OF GOD

> For the preservation of good, for the destruction of
> evil, for the establishment of righteousness, I come
> into being in age after age.
> —*Bhagavad Gita 4:7*

If you walk into the Kwik-E-Mart store in a town called Springfield, you will meet the most well-known Hindu in all of America. His name is Apu Nahasapeemapetilon—originally a PhD in computer science from India, he currently operates a convenience store in the town. He lives in a house adjacent to the store with his wife, Manjula, and their eight children.

Unfortunately, you won't be able to meet this delightful family in person, unless you are a cartoon character. The Nahasapeemapetilons are characters on *The Simpsons*, one of the most popular shows in television history.

There are more than one billion Hindus in the world today, many of them familiar to the Western world—from Mahatma Gandhi to Mindy Kaling.[1] As I write this book, Microsoft and Google, the two major software empires in the world, are headed by CEOs who are Hindus.[2] Yet it is often Apu from the animated world who shapes the popular perception of Hinduism in the West.

According to the Pew Research Center, Hinduism is the third largest religion in the world. But that is merely a statistic. In my opinion, the influence of Hinduism in our culture goes far beyond facts and figures. Let me explain.

Ask random people you meet on the street if they have heard the terms "*yoga*," "*karma*," or "*avatar*." I bet the answer in most cases is going to be "yes." Now ask them if they know what "*lectio divina*," "sanctification," or "incarnation" mean. Most likely they will roll their eyes and say "no." Here is something amusing: the first three words come from the theological vernacular of Hinduism; the last three are the equivalent terms in Christian vocabulary.

In a *Newsweek* article appropriately titled "We Are All Hindus Now," Lisa Miller writes: "America is not a Christian nation.... Recent poll data shows that conceptually, at least, we are slowly becoming more like Hindus and less like traditional Christians in the ways we think about God, ourselves, each other, and eternity." Miller bases her argument on the observations made by Stephen Prothero, professor of religion at Boston University, who also notes that "the American propensity for 'the divine-deli-cafeteria religion'" is "very much in the spirit of Hinduism."[3]

The essence of Hinduism is encapsulated in the phrase "*Sanatana Dharma*," which literally means "Universal Law" or "Universal Duty." In the Hindu worldview, all religions are of the same essence and are different paths to the same destination. A Hindu, therefore, has the freedom to draw elements from any religion, with no need for commitment to a specific doctrine. In other words, Hinduism is more of an amalgamation of different belief systems than it is a credal religion. One is free to pick and choose what he or she wants to believe in this "divine-deli-cafeteria."

○ ○ ○

Julia Roberts, Hollywood actress and American sweetheart, once declared to the press that she was a Hindu. It seemed part of a publicity campaign for one of her movies at the time, but it turns out that Roberts diligently practices her newfound faith even today.[4]

Roberts is not the only celebrity spokesperson for Hinduism in the West. We know that the members of the Beatles often retreated to an ashram in India, submitted to Hindu teachings, and practiced transcendental meditation techniques. They even appointed a Hindu guru, Mahirshi Mahesh Yogi, as their spiritual director. It is also no secret that the founder of Apple, Steve Jobs, ascribed the rediscovery of his life's meaning and purpose to an enlightening spiritual encounter he had in India.

How can a white woman like Julia Roberts, born in the Bible Belt and raised Catholic, suddenly become a Hindu? The fact is that the word *Hindu* literally means a native of India. It is a name the Persian invaders ascribed to the people of the Indus Valley River and beyond. Therefore, the term Hindu indicates a race or ethnicity more than a religion. In that sense, Julia Roberts can never be a Hindu; but I, as a native-born Indian, am one without even realizing it.

Of course, we use the term "Hindu" in a different sense today, to describe the adherents of a religion that we call "Hinduism."

Once again, the irony remains. Hinduism, in reality, is a collective name given to various religious beliefs and practices discovered as part of the Indus Valley civilization, which date all the way back to 3000 BCE.

Hinduism is the only major world religion with no known founder. It is more appropriate to say that the Islamic Emperors of India "invented" the Hindu religion. They used Hinduism as a religious term to distinguish their monotheistic faith from a myriad of polytheistic religions practiced by the indigenous people of the country. For this reason and others, there is no sharp distinction between religion and culture in Hinduism.

It is not that difficult to see how Hinduism has become so seductive to the postmodern sentiments of the Western world. As I mentioned, it is an all-embracing religion, encompassing a wide spectrum of belief systems. It is so universalistic in its ideology that it validates not only the traditional monotheistic and polytheistic beliefs but also a belief in the nonexistence of a personal God. In Hindu thought, all streams of knowledge, including atheism, are genuine paths that will eventually lead us to the Supreme Light.

It can be argued that anyone who believes in virtually anything can be a Hindu. "Whatever celestial form a devotee seeks to worship with faith, I steady the faith of such a devotee in that form," says the Bhagavad Gita, the holy scripture of Hinduism. "Endowed with faith, the devotee worships a particular celestial god and obtains the objects of desire. But in reality I alone arrange these benefits."[5] Judged by this standard, a Christian who is passionately devoted to Christ can be just as good a Hindu as a Muslim who reverently bows before Allah.

Yes, Julia Roberts is a Hindu. But in the true context of Hinduism, so is the pope.

○ ○ ○

The foundational doctrine of Hinduism is something we could describe as "monistic pantheism." It is best encapsulated in the phrase: "All is one; all is God."

To be honest, I have never really understood the meaning of this phrase. Monism argues that God is not "the other"; He/She/It is a Universal Spirit that exists within all of us. You and I are of the same divine essence. I am God; so are you. Pantheism, on the other hand, believes in multiple gods who are characteristically different from each other.

Hinduism is known to the world as an exotic religion with an elaborate pantheon of up to 330 million gods. However, all these gods are various manifestations of one Supreme Consciousness called the *Brahman*. According to the Vedas, the sacred scriptures of Hinduism:

> *Ekam Sat Vipra, Bahuda Vadanti.*[6]
> (That which exists is One; sages call it by various
> names.)

To Hindus, there is only one reality. God and human beings are essentially one and are all part of the same existence. Any apparent distinction between them is caused by a phenomenon called *maya*, or illusion.

The so-called material world we see around us is nothing but a semblance created by maya. The time-space continuum in which we live, and even the appearance of our own individuality, is all part of this illusion. There is neither you nor I; Brahman is all there is. We don't realize this truth because of *avidya* (ignorance), our inability to comprehend the nature of reality.

Avidya is the term in Hindu philosophy that comes closest to what we call "sin" in other religious traditions. Swami Vivekananda once said, "Sinner ... it is a sin to call man so."[7] We are divine souls residing inside physical bodies. We behave inappropriately because we don't realize our divinity. It is not sin we need to overcome, but avidya, in order to eradicate evil and suffering from the world.

According to Hinduism, we are trapped in the epicenter of a grand illusion called the "samsara cycle"—the cycle of birth, death, and rebirth. When a person dies, the soul leaves the body and is reincarnated into a new body. Therefore, our empirical personhood is nothing but an illusion. The moment we realize this truth, we will be "enlightened."

When an enlightened person dies, he or she escapes the samsara cycle and enters *moksha*, a state in which the individual soul merges with the Universal Soul. This absolute union with the individual soul and the Universal Soul is achieved only by renouncing the illusory world in which we live.

According to Hinduism, Jesus was one of these enlightened ones. To them, He displayed the most absolute form of such renunciation, like that of *sadhus*, the wandering holy men of India. Swami Vivekananda described Jesus as a *sannyasi*, an ascetic who withdraws from the pleasures of the material world in order to practice meditation and contemplation.

The time Jesus spent in the wilderness is characteristic of the disciplines of a sadhu. When Jesus said, "I and the Father are one," He was, according to Hindus, speaking of the highest form of mystical union between an individual soul and the Universal Soul that only a holy man can experience.

o o o

I lived in India for well over two decades, but I had never seen a yoga studio until I stepped into one in Chicago. I was there to pick up a friend who was a part-time yoga guru and a part-time real estate agent. He waxed eloquent on the commercial potential of yoga and explained to me how easy it was to make a lucrative income teaching it to the "white folks." I was surprised because, as far as I knew, he had no training in yoga, nor was he an expert in any form of physical or spiritual disciplines. While in college, his athletic abilities were practically as nonexistent as my own.

"I cook up my own version. That is what everybody does," said the guru, with a smirk on his face. "At least I am from India. It gives me credibility."

Perhaps to get rid of his guilt, he later helped me, anonymously, write a proposal for a television documentary on yoga. Our documentary was an exposé of the billion-dollar self-help industry in North America and a satirical look at the transformation of yoga from being a religious ritual in the East to a fitness regimen in the West.

Did I say religious ritual? Yes. That is exactly what true yoga is. The spiritual and the physical are so inextricably blended in yoga that one cannot exist without the other. The word *yoga* itself means "being yoked together." It is a process by which one yokes his or her individual soul with the Universal Soul. The one who achieves this eternal union becomes a *yogi.*

There are predominantly four types of yoga, which are also described as four *margas,* i.e., paths for self-realization and eventual union with the Universal Soul. These two words are often used in conjunction because marga (path) is a means for yoga (union).

What we have been discussing so far is *Raja* or "royal" yoga— a technique that uses psychophysical exercises for invoking the dormant psychic energy within us to unite our human and divine natures. In addition to Raja, another type of yoga is *Karma* yoga, or the path to union through action or work.

The key concept behind this form of yoga is that of *nishkama* karma (disinterested action), whereby one's duty is performed with no concern about its consequences. "He who does the task dictated by duty, caring nothing for the fruit of action, he is a yogi," says Lord Krishna.[8] Whatever we do with a selfish motive adds an extra layer to our ego, thereby further removing us from the Universal Soul. On the other hand, every selfless deed we perform removes a layer of ego, until there is no barrier that separates us from the divine.[9]

Neither Karma yoga nor Raja yoga mandates the recognition of God or any divine figures in religious practice. In order to understand the concept of God in Hinduism, therefore, we need to go to the next two margas: *Jnana* yoga (the path of knowledge) and *Bhakti* yoga (the path of devotion).

o o o

"Where is God? How can I see Him?" a son asks his father.

The father hands him a pinch of salt. He then asks him to go and mix it in a cup of water. "Where is the salt now?" asks the father.

"I cannot see it. The salt and water have become one."

"As the salt is in the water, we are one with the Universal Spirit. Just as there is no difference between the salt and the water, there is no difference between you and God. Thou art That!"

The above is a popular story from the Hindu Upanishads, which are commentaries to the Vedas.[10] The phrase "Thou art That" (*Tat tvam Asi*) defines the foundational principle of Jnana yoga, the path to union with the Universal Soul through knowledge.

Jnana yoga conceives of God as a formless Self with no personal attributes, often called *Nirguna* Brahman. God is not a He or a She but a "That"—a transcendent reality that encompasses everything that exists in the universe. The essence of Brahman is *Satchitananda*: infinite being (*Sat*), infinite consciousness (*Chit*), and infinite bliss (*Ananda*).

If the Universal Soul is Brahman, an individual soul is called *atman*. The realization that the atman and the Brahman are the same ("*Aham Brahma Asmi*," or "I am Brahman")[11] brings "enlightenment." Enlightenment leads to moksha at death, where the atman is liberated from the samsara cycle and eternally merged into Brahman.

Jnana yoga generally stands against all forms of worship and devotion. Salvation comes from within; we do not need the help of a deity to achieve moksha. In other words, we are our own saviors.

Even though there are no savior figures in the Jnana yoga tradition, there are spiritual guides available to help us on our path to enlightenment and, eventually, to moksha. Such a guide is called a *guru*.

A guru is more than a teacher or an expert; for an aspirant, he is the conduit to divinity. He not only imparts knowledge, but also embodies it. The students are taught to recite the popular mantra "*matha pitha guru daivatam*," on the first day of their school, which literally means, "Mother, Father, and Teacher are to be revered as gods themselves." The relationship between a guru and his students, therefore, closely resembles that of a deity and the devotees in other streams of Hinduism.

○ ○ ○

While philosophical Hinduism remains a hot topic in intellectual discourses, most Hindus follow devotional Hinduism, which, like most other religions, involves worshipping personal deities and observing religious rituals. Armchair philosophers may have the luxury to sit and contemplate the nature of cosmic illusion, but ordinary people live in the real world, and they need real solutions to real problems. No religion, therefore, can survive without personal gods who could answer the prayers of the devotees.

This is where Bhakti yoga, the path to union through devotion, finds its way into the religious landscape of Hinduism. The god of Bhakti yoga is not an impersonal Absolute but a Supreme Person. He is not the Nirguna Brahman of Jnana yoga but the *Saguna* Brahman, God with personal attributes:

With eyes on all sides and mouths on all sides,
With arms on all sides and feet on all sides,
The One God created the sky and the earth,
Fanning them with his arms.[12]

The Saguna Brahman is not the apathetic, immutable Universal Soul of the Jnana yoga; he is a "person" interested in entering into a meaningful relationship with his creation. He interacts with his devotees in an intimately personal way, calling them into a loving relationship with him:

Always think of me, be devoted to me,
Worship me, and offer obeisance to me.
Doing so, you will certainly come to me.
This is my pledge to you, for you are very dear to me.[13]

What prevents the devotees from entering into this relationship is not avidya; rather, it is their personal offenses, akin to what we call "sin" in other religions. The worshippers can appeal to the love of god, relating to him as a father, a friend, or even as a lover:

As a father tolerates his son,
A friend forgives his friend, and
A lover pardons the beloved,
Please forgive me for my offences.[14]

In Hindu mythology, this one god, often called *Iswara* or *Bhagavan*,[15] manifests himself in the form of three distinct personal gods: Brahma (notice the difference between this and *Brahman*), Vishnu, and Siva. Together they are called the *Trimurthy*. As the sacred scriptures suggest, "the Supreme Spirit hath three conditions. In the form of Brahma, he is the Creator, and in the form of Vishnu, he is the Preserver, and in his form as Rudra (Siva), he is the Destroyer of the Universe!"[16] Iswara is constantly engaged in the action of creation, preservation, and destruction through the Trimurthy.[17]

Although the concept of Trimurthy sounds very similar to the Christian idea of a Triune God, these theologies are very different. In the Trinity, one divine nature expresses itself in three distinct persons. But in Trimurthy, the one being manifests itself as three individual gods who operate independently of each other.

Bhakti yoga believes in God's "otherness" from the rest of the creation. If one needs to be devoted to God, God cannot be oneself. In other words, the creator and the creation have to be distinct entities, connected through a loving relationship between them. In Jnana yoga, Brahman and atman are depicted as the ocean and the waves rippling over its surface; they are one and the same. But in Jnana yoga, Brahman and atman are like the ocean and the many rivers that are flowing toward it. They have distinct identities until the blissful union is achieved.

o o o

The legendary filmmaker James Cameron wrote and directed one of the highest-grossing films of all time, *Avatar*.[18] Not many people know that the word *avatar* comes straight from the theological dictionary of Hinduism. It originates from a Sanskrit word that means "to descend." In Hindu scriptures, an *avatar* represents the descent of God from the spiritual world into the material world.

This is exactly what the protagonist does in the movie *Avatar*. The paraplegic US Marine Jake Sully enters the genetically engineered body of a "Na'vi" and lives among them on planet Pandora. Jake exists in two realities at the same time: his human body is inside a giant teleporter in the human camp, but his alien avatar lives in the Na'vi community.

In Christian lexicon, the word *avatar* is translated "incarnation." Christianity and Hinduism are the only two major religions that believe in the doctrine of incarnation. For Jews and Muslims, to picture God as human is sacrilegious. And it is inconceivable for Buddhists and Sikhs. In most religious traditions, God is a transcendent entity who is never described in anthropomorphic terms. But in Christianity and in Hinduism, God is immanent—He manifests Himself in a physical body. He can exist in both the finite and the infinite at the same time, just like Jake Sully in *Avatar*.

The descents of Vishnu are collectively called *Dashavatar* or the "ten incarnations."[19] Rama and Krishna are the two most popular and commonly worshipped avatars in Hindu religion. A Hindu is encouraged to "live as Rama lived, learn what Krishna taught."[20]

Krishna is depicted as a romantic figure engaged in *rasalila* (love game) with his beloved Radha and her *gopis* (maids). Radha is Krishna's supreme beloved; she becomes one with him through pure love. Their relationship mirrors God's affinity to humanity: "The love of Radha and Krishna is symbolic of the eternal love affair between the devoted mortal and the Divine," says Swami Chinmayananda. "Radha's yearning for union with her beloved

Krishna is the soul's longing for spiritual awakening to be united with the one Source of peace and bliss from which it has become separated."[21]

This romantic undertone in the relationship between the deity and the devotee in Bhakti yoga resonates deeply within the core theology of Christianity. The Bible, at times, portrays God almost as a "hopeless romantic" yearning for the love of His people. Jesus is a bridegroom who is betrothed to the church and looks forward to the heavenly marriage to take place in the coming world.[22] In Bhakti tradition and in Christianity, therefore, religion is more of a romantic affair between the divine and the human than meticulous observance of rules and regulations.

The final avatar of Vishnu is Kalkin, the tenth and the last of the Dashavatar. He has yet to manifest. Kalkin is the apocalyptic messiah who will arrive at the end of this epoch (*Yuga*). The Hindu scriptures describe his impending appearance in vivid details, in a manner strikingly similar to that of the second coming of Jesus in the book of Revelation:

> At the end of Kali Yuga,
>   when there exist no topics on the subject of God,
>   even at the residences of so-called saints
>   and respectable gentlemen,
>   and when the power of government
>   is transferred to the hands of
>   ministers elected from the evil men,
>   and when nothing is known of
>   the techniques of sacrifice,

the Lord will appear as

the supreme chastiser.[23]

Kalkin is portrayed in Indian art as a king riding on a white horse with a silver sword in his hands. On the last day he will execute judgment on all creation. He will then reset the cosmic clock, announcing the birth of a new era. The *Kali Yuga* (Age of Vices) will end, and *Satya Yuga* (Age of Truth) will commence. As written in the book of Revelation, "I saw a new heaven and a new earth; for the first heaven and the first earth passed away.... Behold, I am making all things new."[24]

A Hindu would have no qualms about accepting Jesus as a perfect avatar, similar to Lord Krishna or Lord Kalkin. But for Christians, the uniqueness of Jesus Christ is of paramount importance. He is not one of many avatars; He is the only one. Christians in India describe Him as "the only avatar," "the abiding avatar," and "the historical avatar."[25]

o o o

One of the fondest memories from my childhood is the celebration of Onam, a religious festival widely celebrated in the southern part of India. The story behind Onam fascinates me even today, because in this tale, God plays the role of a villain.

Once upon a time, a king named Mahabali reigned over Kerala, the Indian state where I was born. This era was a golden age, where peace and prosperity prevailed in abundant measure. The lyrics of a popular folk song capture it in vivid detail:

> When Mahabali ruled the land, all people enjoyed
> equal status and were extremely happy. None had
> any difficulty, and there was no disease or decay.
> Infant mortality was unknown during the time,
> and the people enjoyed a long life.[26]

According to Hindu mythology, the gods who inhabited the heavenly world became jealous, and they conceived a devious plan to trick Mahabali. The Lord Vishnu appeared in the form of a dwarf (Vamana, one of the ten incarnations), and pleaded with the king to grant him three feet of land for performing a sacrifice ritual (*yajna*). The generous king happily obliged and granted him this modest wish.

The moment Mahabali made the promise, the unthinkable happened: Vamana's body grew into gigantic proportions and filled the universe. With one foot, he measured the whole earth, and with the next, he measured the heavens. Now there was no place left to measure the third foot.

In order to honor his promise, Mahabali bowed his head so that Vamana could measure his third foot on his body. Vamana lowered his foot on the head of the king and pushed him all the way down into the netherworld. Mahabali's unwavering commitment to his promise pleased Vamana, however, so he granted the king permission to return to his kingdom once every year.

"Onam" is the day when the king returns from the underworld to visit his subjects.

What intrigues me the most in this story is the name of the king, Mahabali, because it means "the great sacrifice."

The ritual of sacrifice is an all-pervasive sacrament in Hindu religion. Yajna (sacrifice) in itself is seen as the "very essence of the Vedas," says a Hindu doctrine. "From the early times, the ritual was understood to be the link between the human and the divine and a vehicle towards liberation."[27] Today, blood sacrifices are not practical due to various governmental regulations. Therefore, most Hindus have an altar in their house where they offer food, milk, and other gifts to their favorite deities.

In the Christian story, God metaphorically measures the heavens and the earth, only to encounter the infinite chasm that separates them. Jesus stands in the middle, bridging the gap between these divided worlds. He accepts the inevitable third foot, the measure of judgment, on Himself and becomes the *mahabali*, i.e., the great sacrifice. With His death, He conquered death. With His sacrifice, He produced eternal life. Like Mahabali, He rose from the grave and came back to live among His people. He will be coming back again to establish the eternal kingdom characterized by peace and prosperity.

O O O

Sacrifice is a central theme of the Hindu scriptures. According to the Vedas, the universe came into existence through the sacrifice of a deity, Prajapati (Lord of Creatures), who appears as the creator god in the Rig Veda: "O Prajapati, none other than thou encompasses all these creatures; for whatever object of desire we sacrifice to thee, let that be ours; may we be lords of riches."[28]

I remember visiting a "church" dedicated to Prajapati in northern India.[29] It looked more like an apartment building in the midst of a busy residential enclave. The hall was saturated with the aroma of burning incense. Melodic chants of sacred mantras filled the air. To my surprise, I found something that looked like an altar in the middle of the room, and a statue of Jesus placed on it.

"We are Hindus who worship Prajapati," said the priest. "We believe Jesus of Nazareth was the historical fulfillment of the Prajapati myth in Hinduism. He is the creator God who revealed Himself in history."

Conventional Christians in India view Prajapati worship as a dangerous cult. However, as I dug deeper, the resemblances between Jesus and Prajapati became overwhelmingly obvious. One of the unique attributes of Prajapati, for example, is that he is half-human and half-divine. "Now, one half of that Prajapati was mortal, and the other half immortal," says the Upanishads. "With that part of him which was mortal he was afraid of death; and, being afraid, he became twofold, clay and water, and entered this [earth]."[30] This paradoxical combination of divinity and humanity is the first thing that comes to mind when we think of Jesus.

Prajapati is believed to be the one who established the ritual of sacrifice in order to commemorate a sacrifice he himself performed with his own body at the beginning of time. The Rig Veda describes this Prajapati yajna as an act in which Prajapati (also called Purusha, the primordial man) sacrificially dismembered his body to create the world.[31] "Prajapati is sacrifice," says a Upanishad. "For he created it in his own self-expression."[32]

A sacrifice may be performed for various reasons, whether to appease the gods or to atone for one's sins. But the true sacrifice is the Prajapati himself. "And indeed, there was no other victim meant for sacrifice but that one Prajapati. They did offer him up. These were the first ordinances."[33]

The sacrifice of his own body did not kill Prajapati; it rather made him immortal. With his death the sacrificial man created life and returned to it.[34] "Prajapati became immortal; and in like manner does the Sacrificer become immortal by making that body [on the altar] immortal."[35]

The priest explained to me in great detail how different aspects of the Prajapati yajna were manifested in the crucifixion of Jesus Christ. "Taken in its totality, the myth of the Purusha/Prajapati is not unworthy of the Christian conception of the redemptive incarnation of the logos (Word = Jesus)," says Augilar, a Hindu scholar.[36] Jesus, like Prajapati, is the One who was "slain from the foundation of the world."[37] In Jesus, God presents Himself as the perfect and sufficient sacrifice for human iniquities. His death atones for our sins and restores our broken relationship with God, thus fulfilling the true meaning of yajna.

o o o

According to Jnana tradition of Hinduism, Jesus is an enlightened guru who taught humanity how to walk the path to moksha. In that sense, He is the personification of the divine itself and is often addressed as *gurudeva* (the guru god). Jesus can help us overcome the evil of ignorance (*avidya*) and find the true path to enlightenment.

Followers of Karma yoga accept Jesus as a great moral teacher, and often quote the Sermon on the Mount in their ethical discourses. Great social reformers of India, such as Raja Ram Mohan Roy and Mahatma Gandhi, were inspired by the idea of *ahimsa* (nonviolence) in Jesus' teachings and incorporated it in their social justice campaigns.

According to Bhakti tradition, Jesus is an avatar—the incarnation of God—almost similar to who He is in Christianity. But the purpose of incarnation is diametrically opposed in both traditions. According to Bhagavad Gita, an avatar appears in the world to destroy sinners and deliver saints:

> Whenever there is a decline in righteousness
> And an increase in unrighteousness,
> O Arjun, at that time I manifest myself on earth.
> To protect the righteous, to annihilate the wicked,
> And to reestablish the principles of dharma
> I appear on this earth, age after age.[38]

Jesus, on the other hand, "did not come to call the righteous, but sinners."[39] Unlike the other avatars, Jesus was known as a "friend of the sinners." He repeatedly affirmed, "The Son of Man has come to seek and to save that which was lost."[40]

Only in Christianity and Hinduism does God appear in human form. But in Hinduism, the mission of God is retribution, whereas in Christianity, it is reconciliation. While the god of Hinduism will have to come to this world age after age to execute retributive justice, Jesus came once for all and accomplished His reconciliatory mission on the cross.

Jake Sully's story in *Avatar* finds its parallel in the Jesus story of the Bible. Sully came to planet Pandora proclaiming the imminent arrival of a different kingdom. He was commissioned to aid in a military campaign against the Na'vi, but instead he strove to negotiate peace. In the end, the chastiser became the deliverer, paid the price of salvation with his own life, and resurrected into the new reality as the ultimate savior.

The salvific mission of Jesus on the cross can be framed within the theology of yajna in Hinduism. "The Vedic conception of sin is analogous to the Hebrew theory," noted S. Radha Krishnan, a prominent Hindu scholar who was once the president of India. "It is a consciousness of sin that calls for propitiatory sacrifices."[41] Mahatma Gandhi, who epitomizes Hinduism to the modern mind, once described Jesus as "a man who was completely innocent, offered himself as a sacrifice for the good of others, including his enemies, and became the ransom of the world."[42]

John Nicole Farquhar, an early Scottish missionary to India, studied the parallel themes in Hindu mythology and Christian theology and arrived at the conclusion that Christianity is the "evolutionary crown" of Hinduism. "Every important Christian truth is foreshadowed in Hinduism," said Farquhar. "The task of the Christian worker is to discover these and indicate how they are fulfilled in Christ."[43] Sadhu Sunder Singh, the legendary Christian sage of India, believed that Hinduism had been preparing the way for Christianity to enter the religious consciousness of the country. "Hinduism has been digging channels," said Singh. "Christ is the water to flow through these channels."

As a Christian journeying through Hinduism, I find these religions occupying opposite ends of the theological spectrum: one is pantheistic, the other monotheistic; one fluid with many forms of worship and connections to God, the other seemingly dogmatic with only one way to Him. Yet upon closer inspection, the faces of the savior figure emerging from them are not so far apart. In both religions, the infinite God enters the finite world as "Immanuel," the One who is with us. He performs the ultimate yajna for our redemption, and courts us into a (romantic) relationship with Him.

What if the God of the Bible, in His infinite grace, had chosen to reveal His descent into the world to my Hindu ancestors? I begin to wonder.

The Star of the Savior shines brighter even in the darkness that swoops in to overpower the light. The folk song of the religious festival Onam continues at a distance, reminiscing the glorious days of the Great King:

> No one said a lie,
> There was no theft or deceit,
> Measures and weights were right;
> No one wronged his neighbor.
> When Mahabali ruled the land,
> All the people were regarded equal.

Thy kingdom come, I pray.

Chapter 3

THE SUFFERING SAVIOR

I take upon myself the burden of all suffering....
At all costs I must bear the burdens of all beings.
In that I do not follow my own inclinations. I have
made the vow to save all beings. All beings I must
set free.

—*Sikshasamuccaya, 280–81 (Vajradhvaja Sutra)[1]*

Seinfeld, a popular sitcom on American television, famously described itself as a "show about nothing"—a phrase that has since become a meme in popular culture. In an episode titled "The Pitch," Jerry Seinfeld and George Costanza pitch a new television show to a group of studio executives.[2]

"I think I can sum up the show for you with one word," says George with a contemplative pause.

"Nothing."

"Nothing? What does that mean?" asks the befuddled executive.

"Nothing happens on the show. See, it's just like life!"

As irreverent as *Seinfeld* itself might be, in curious ways this tagline strikes a deep chord of resonance with the futility of our collective search for the meaning of life.

It also reflects the existential vacuum at the very heart of the religion we call Buddhism.

As we explore this religion, the first thing that will take us by surprise is the fact that the concept of God does not exist in it—neither the impersonal Brahman nor the personal Iswara. *Isn't Buddha the god of Buddhism?* one might wonder. No, he is not. It turns out that we are all endowed with the Buddha nature, and we all have the potential to become Buddha ourselves.

A religion without God does not make sense to many; yet it is nothing new to the culture in which I was born and raised. Most Eastern religions incorporate a healthy respect for nontheistic traditions such as agnosticism, and even atheism, within their wide spectrum of religious beliefs.

What is more perplexing about Buddhism is its understanding of the personal soul—which, by the way, does not exist either. "The individual has no real core," says Buddhism.[3] While Hinduism describes humans as embodied souls or atman (self), Buddhism considers us *anatman*, or "no-self." Our personality is "constantly changing" and "the idea of an immortal soul is simply an illusion that human beings impose on a process of constant change."[4]

We are all nothing but a combination of cells, nerves, and blood animated by a stream of conscience. Identity is an illusion created by five components, *skandhas*—physical body, sensation, perception, cognition, and consciousness—that come together for a specific period of time. At the time of death, skandhas disperse into a "flux" and blend with other skandhas to form a new sentient being.[5]

In essence, our identity is similar to that of a car in which the mechanical components—the tires, brakes, engine, transmission system, and so on—come together to form an entity we perceive as a car. In reality all that exists are the components; the idea of a car in and of itself is an illusion.

To put it bluntly, life is a show about nothing.

There is no God; there is no personal soul. All that really exists is "void" or emptiness.

Buddhism is the *Seinfeld* of world religions—a show that deconstructs human life into a series of random processes, which devolves into "nothing."

○ ○ ○

Siddhartha Gautama was an Indian prince who lived in fifth century BCE.[6] His father, King Suddhodana, was the ruler of Kapilavastu, which is part of modern-day Nepal. Siddhartha married his cousin Yasodhara when they were both teenagers. The couple soon had a son, Rahula, who would be their only child.

Life seemed to be going well until one day when Siddhartha stepped outside the palace and came face to face with the harsh realities of a suffering world. The mortality of life and the meaninglessness of its existence haunted the prince. Leaving his wife and child behind, Siddhartha embarked on a spiritual journey. His goal was to find a solution to the problem of suffering.

Siddhartha was only twenty-nine years old when he left the palace. At first, he joined a group of Hindu sadhus, who taught him the path of renunciation and esoteric meditation techniques. After six years of intense ascetic life, he had a profound spiritual encounter, which came to be known as his "enlightenment." While meditating under a tree, Siddhartha came to the realization that the austerity of a monk is just as meaningless as the self-indulgence of a prince. The path to liberation, he concluded, is the "middle way"— a life that neither denies nor indulges in the pleasures of the world.

This realization awakened the Buddha nature in Siddhartha, and he came to be known as the Buddha, or "the awakened one." Buddha then established the *sangha*, a community of monks dedicated to carrying his message of the middle way across the world. He continued his teaching for another four decades, and at age eighty, died of accidental food poisoning.

Buddha's solution to the problem of suffering is summarized in his teaching of the "four noble truths":

The first noble truth states the thesis: "All is suffering."

The second truth identifies the problem: "Desire is the root cause of suffering."

The third truth promises a solution: "Suffering has an end."

The fourth truth attempts to frame a solution to the problem of suffering in the form of an "eightfold path": "Right view, right resolve, right speech, right conduct, right occupation, right effort, right awareness, and right meditation."

A life lived according to this guideline is following the "the middle way."

The eightfold path certainly points us to a noble way to live our lives, but one might wonder how to understand the word "right" that appears in all its propositions. If we do not believe in God, there is no absolute moral standard against which we can measure right and wrong. If everyone is left to decide what is right or wrong for themselves, the eightfold path, while intending to eradicate suffering, may unintentionally become a perpetrator of it.

The closer we get, the more we realize that the concept of nothingness is at the very center of the Buddhist solution to the problem of suffering. Even the experience of suffering is not real; it is an illusion. The only way out of our existential crisis is that of withdrawal from the perceived physical reality and transcendence into the world of emptiness.

o o o

The book of Ecclesiastes is undoubtedly the biblical text that resonates most with the core ideology of Buddhism. King Solomon, after setting his mind on seeking and exploring "all that has been done under heaven" comes to a devastating conclusion: "'Vanity of vanities,' says the Preacher, 'Vanity of vanities! All is vanity.'"[7]

Buddhism ultimately brings us to the same conclusion. Consider the following exchange from a source that, while perhaps less profound than the book of Ecclesiastes, still illuminates essential truths: *The Simpsons.*

In an episode titled "She of Little Faith," Lisa Simpson walks into Springfield's Buddhist temple. Hollywood actor Richard Gere, a self-proclaimed Buddhist, is raking the Zen garden inside the temple. He gives Lisa a pamphlet that explains the basic precepts of Buddhism.

"All things are impermanent and are empty of inherent existence," Richard tells Lisa.

"'Positive actions lead to happiness and negative actions lead to unhappiness,'" Lisa reads aloud to herself in her room later. There is no better way to summarize Buddhism in under ten seconds.

In a world with no God and no individual souls, all that really exists is *shunya*, or emptiness. Even the ultimate liberation that Buddhism promises, *nirvana*, is nothing but a complete annihilation of life itself.

Buddhism subscribes to the reincarnation theory of Hinduism, but it does not clearly say what is actually being reincarnated. Hinduism has the concept of atman—a personal soul, the identity of which can be theoretically conceived. But a Buddhist anatman is not an individual soul, only a sentient energy, which will eventually disappear into a psychic flux when the skandhas separate at the time of death.

If that is the case, how does my karma follow me? Where am "I" anyway? Why should I care about what "I" do if the "I" itself does not exist?

The problem becomes even more serious at the end of the reincarnation cycle where the sentient being achieves "nirvana." What is nirvana? It is a mode of existence very similar to moksha in Hinduism, where the atman becomes one with Brahman. But what does nirvana look like if there is no atman or Brahman?

Buddha himself was unable to answer questions on the true nature of nirvana. He told his disciples that only those who experience nirvana could really understand what it is. Instead of trying to speculate what nirvana is, he said, they should concentrate on striving to achieve it.

Nirvana is "a kind of gnosis, or direct apprehension of truth, which deepens over time and eventually reaches full maturity in the complete awakening experienced by the Buddha," says one Buddhist scholar.[8] It is a "fusion of virtue and wisdom," says another. Yet another scholar describes it as a "transformed state of personality characterized by peace, deep spiritual joy, compassion and a refined and subtle awareness."[9] As profound as these explanations seem to appear, they are nothing but the crafty words of accomplished wordsmiths. In reality, nirvana is nothing but pure emptiness, or *shunya*.

The theory of emptiness in Buddhism produces a nihilist worldview, pushing us to the brink of a moral abyss. The theory of vanity in the book of Ecclesiastes, in contrast, lands on a completely different note. "The conclusion, when all has been heard, is: fear God and keep His commandments, because this applies to every person," says Ecclesiastes. "For God will bring every act to judgment, everything which is hidden, whether it is good or evil."[10]

Prince Siddhartha and King Solomon made the same observations but they arrived at dramatically different conclusions. To one, nothing matters; to the other, everything does.

Rob Johnston, professor of theology and culture at Fuller Seminary, uses the book of Ecclesiastes as a lens to interpret the elements of redemptive revelations in popular culture. He often states an aphorism in the class, which summarizes the message of the book beautifully: "Life sucks, but it is wonder-filled."

Life in Siddhartha's world sucks because it is empty and void. The life in Solomon's world also sucks; yet the presence of God instills it with beauty, wonder, and meaning.

○ ○ ○

There are no central authority figures in Buddhism. The Dalai Lama is often considered the spokesperson of Buddhism in the West, but in reality, he represents only a small group of Buddhists who are part of the *Vajrayana* ("diamond vehicle") tradition, which most others consider a heretical sect.

Although he presents himself as a charismatic monk in popular media, in reality, the Dalai Lama leads an occult religion that borrows from tantric Hinduism and Tibetan shamanism. His version of Buddhism incorporates many esoteric rituals and psychic experiments from other religious texts, including the Tibetan "Book of the Dead" and Indian "Forbidden Veda,"[11] into Buddhist practice. He is revered in Tibet as the manifestation of a celestial Buddha, whose title is being passed on from one life to the next through the reincarnation cycle.[12]

There are many schools of teaching in Buddhism that emerged out of the schisms that sprang up in the community immediately after Buddha's death. In a council that met not long after his passing, the sangha split into *Theravada* (doctrine of elders)—a conservative faction that stuck to the original teachings of Buddha—and *Mahayana* (great vehicle)—a liberal wing, which argued that the only way for survival was to adapt to the traditions of indigenous religions. Theravada claims an unbroken lineage of monks that extends all the way back to Buddha. Mahayana, on the other hand, de-emphasizes the historical Buddha and argues that all aspirants will become Buddhas at some point in time.

The most popular form of Buddhism in the Western world is Zen Buddhism, which integrates Japanese martial arts into Buddhist meditation techniques. It focuses not on philosophical discourses, but on "mindfulness," making us aware of the timelessness of ordinary moments. The Zen masters create a "quickening" of the spirit (*satori* experience) through mind-bending puzzles known as *koan*[13] or through aesthetic experiences ranging from flower arrangements to landscaping. The stunning landscapes of Zen gardens remind us of the tranquility and serenity of each passing moment, whereas Zen meditation techniques invoke a profound sense of quietness and stillness to our "inner landscape."

Buddhism is growing rapidly in the Western world today. It appeals to the scientific worldview of modernity, which portrays life as a meaningless compilation of atoms and molecules animated by a series of chemical rules. At the same time, it also plays into the spiritual sensibilities of postmodernity by offering us an opportunity to become "spiritual" without being "religious." You get the best of both worlds.

A few American Buddhists are now calling for a "*Navayana*" (new vehicle) Buddhism, one that "blends with the best of Western science, psychology and social science…. Its forms must ever change to serve the ever-changing human need."[14] It is this mastery of adaptability that makes Buddhism one of the most favored religions in the West.

o o o

I never had an opportunity to meet a Buddhist while I lived in India. I think one has a better chance of running into a suit-wearing Mormon missionary in India than a saffron-wearing Buddhist monk.

It is a cold irony that a religion that has spread its wings and flown across the world has become an endangered species in its birthplace. Why would a country that holds no bars against any religion turn its back on one of its own?

This is of particular interest considering the fact that Buddhism is, and always has been, a missionary religion. Buddha traveled across India as an itinerant missionary, teaching his message over a span of forty years (as opposed to less than four years in the case of Jesus). On his deathbed, he commissioned sixty elders to take his message all over the world (as opposed to the twelve apostles of Jesus).

The people of India, however, rejected Buddhism simply because it contributed nothing new to offer to their already satu-rated religious souls. The highly touted Buddhist philosophy, as far as the Hindus were concerned, was just a remix of their own philosophical propositions. So when Buddha's disciples went around preaching the middle way, Indians saw the new religion as nothing but "Hinduism lite." As one of my Hindu friends says, "If Buddha claims to have established a new religion, Hindus will file for copyright infringement."

Buddhist missionaries soon left India and traveled north-ward to China, Korea, and Japan. The people of these countries welcomed them, assuming that they were Hindu monks from India. The predominant religions in this region at the time were

Confucianism and Taoism. Confucianism was a set of socio-ethical principles and Taoism was a way to live in harmony with nature; neither had much to say about gods or afterlife. The people of Asia expected Buddhist missionaries to bring them an unlimited supply of gods and goddesses from Hinduism.

The monks exploited this opportunity and devised a "folk version" of Buddhism, tailor-made to the needs of the god-starved masses of Asia. In order to outshine humanistic Confucianism and mystical Taoism, they imported magic and mantras from Hinduism. Although Buddhist doctrines affirmed there was no God, the missionaries borrowed as many gods and goddesses as they could from the Hindu pantheon. They encouraged the devotees to worship Buddha as God Himself, and other deities as his various manifestations.[15]

Buddhism adopted the same strategy even as it entered the West. Individualism and scientific rationalism were the dominant ideologies of the time; so the missionaries incorporated self-help theories and empowerment ideologies to their doctrines. As a scholar wisely noted, "the fact that Buddhism imposes few confessional, ritual or other requirements on its followers makes it easy to live as a Buddhist in a pluralistic milieu and minimizes the likelihood of overt conflict with secular values."[16] A religion that started as a reformed version of Hinduism in the East thus became a baptized version of scientific humanism in the West.[17]

The new and improved version of Buddhism in North America is an esoteric mix of atheism and New Age spirituality. "Buddhism teaches the way to perfect goodness and wisdom without a personal God; the highest knowledge without a revelation ... the possibility of redemption without a vicarious redeemer," says a Buddhist monk. It is "a salvation in which everyone is his own savior."[18] Why do we need God if we can design our own salvation? Why surrender to Him if we can be the masters of our own destiny?

What a tempting offer!

o o o

I sat on a wooden bench in Deer Park at Saranath, a city in the northern part of India. Although Buddha was born in Kapilavasthu, Buddhism was born here in Saranath. This is where Buddha preached his first sermon, laying out the four noble truths.

I had a clear view of the *Dhamekh Stupa*, a cylindrical coffin in which Buddha's remains rest. A group of barefooted monks walked around it chanting *dharma sutras*. The visitors, mostly tourists from other South Asian countries, marched behind them. Some of them kissed the Stupa and sprinkled it with incense and flower petals. The prayers they muttered were choked in tears.

The Buddhism I saw in Saranath was quite different from the Buddhism I learned from watching *The Simpsons*. The Buddhists I saw in India were like followers of any other religion. They were passionate devotees of a transcendent deity. They believed in god(s), and they were certainly concerned about their personal soul.

This is what "real" Buddhism looks like in most parts of the world. What we know of Buddhism from the Western media is a far cry from what is often practiced in Buddhist temples across the world. Buddhism is considered a pantheistic religion in the majority world, as most Buddhists worship gods, and some even demons.

The monks function as priests, exercising ecclesiastical authority over congregations. As a Buddhist scholar observes, "Buddhists have familiar patterns of ritual and worship. They go on pilgrimages to important shrines; they worship images and sites that are sacred to Buddha; and they mark the stages of life with rites of passage."[19]

Ordinary Buddhists do not even care about nirvana; they rather hope for an afterlife free of suffering, reunited with their loved ones. Japanese Buddhists, for example, imagine a celestial paradise, "Pure Land," where gods and goddesses reside. This paradise is described in material terms, and its description closely resembles the "new heaven" described in the book of Revelation:

> Land of Ultimate Bliss is everywhere surrounded by seven tiers of railings, seven layers of netting, and seven rows of trees, all formed from the four treasures.... It has pools of the seven jewels, filled with the eight waters of merit and virtue.... On the four sides are stairs of gold, silver, lapis lazuli, and crystal; above are raised pavilions adorned with gold, silver, lapis lazuli, crystal, mother-of-pearl, red pearls, and carnelian. In the pools are lotuses as large as carriage wheels.... In that Buddha land there is always heavenly music ... there are always rare and wonderful varicolored birds.... In the six periods of the day and night the flocks of birds sing forth harmonious and elegant sounds.... Those living beings who hear should vow, "I wish to be born in that country." And why? Those who thus

attain are all superior and good people, all coming
together in one place.[20]

In the same vein, there are also multiple levels of "hell" in
Buddhism. There are cold hells where people are tortured by freez-
ing, and hot hells where they are roasted in fire. The only good news
about the Buddhist hell is that it is not a place of eternal damnation.
People will be released from hell once they finish paying for all their
bad karma.

A Western Buddhist may consider these beliefs to be credulous
or superstitious, but it is the real Buddhism practiced in most parts
of the world and the only type of Buddhism that has stood the test
of time. A religion without God can be a great topic of conversation
for armchair philosophers, but it will have no power to address the
"felt needs" of ordinary people.

○ ○ ○

The Matrix, the 1999 blockbuster directed by the Wachowski
brothers, was a benchmark film that set new standards for style and
storytelling in Hollywood. One of the unique attributes of the film
that many critics gravitated toward was its philosophical undertone.
The Matrix resonated with the spiritual sensibilities of the view-
ers. Some even described watching the film as an "enlightening"
experience.

The story of *The Matrix* has interesting parallels to the Buddhist
narrative of the universe. The film suggests that we live in a virtual
world—what we see with our eyes and hear with our ears exists only

in our imagination. It is an illusion created by an artificial intelligence. Consider the similarities to the Buddhist world, where we are imprisoned within an illusory matrix created by our own karmic impressions.

The hero of *The Matrix* is a computer hacker named Neo who manages to break through the walls of the matrix and enter the realm of reality. This is what liberation looks like in Buddhism. A true Buddha leaps over the walls of the samsara cycle and enters the realm of nirvana.

The Matrix does not stop with liberation, however. Neo comes back to the matrix as an enlightened savior. He is the fulfillment of a prophecy. He is the One they have been waiting for!

Is there such a savior figure in Buddhism? Apparently, the answer is yes. This savior figure is called a *bodhisattva.*

The bodhisattva, like Neo, attains nirvana but chooses to come back to the samsara instead of remaining in the realm of nirvana. He continues in the reincarnation cycle without passing into absolute Buddhahood. He will become Buddha only when his mission on earth is accomplished.

A bodhisattva, therefore, is a "Buddha-to-be." All bodhisattvas will one day become Buddha. Until then, they postpone their own nirvana in order to help others achieve enlightenment. They are, therefore, the ultimate symbol of compassion, which is the supreme virtue in Buddhism.

Bodhisattvas possess superhuman abilities to switch between their appearances. They can also travel between the heavenly and earthly realms. Each time they reach heaven, however, the bodhisattvas decide to return to the world for the sake of others. This mission requires great suffering and sacrifice on their part.[21]

Siddhartha is believed to be one such bodhisattva who came back from nirvana to teach us what we now know as Buddhism. "Although the historical Buddha had appeared to live and die like an ordinary man, he had, in reality, been enlightened from time immemorial," notes a scholar. "As a wise and compassionate teacher, however, he had gone through an elaborate charade to accommodate the expectations of the people of the time."[22]

Today, bodhisattvas have become the Buddhist equivalent of Hindu gods. According to scholars, "the cult of bodhisattvas ... promised not just rebirth in another world, but in direct assistance with the concern of this life, such as the birth of a child or prosperity in the family."[23] Worshippers picture bodhisattvas as celestial beings with mythological attributes or as human beings with supernatural powers. They often are venerated as deities in Buddhist temples and local shrines.

The bodhisattva who is popular in Japan is Amida/Amidaba (Buddha of Infinite Light), the custodian of Pure Land. Those who have enough good karma can choose to be reborn into this paradise instead of entering nirvana. In Pure Land, they also have the option to go back to the earthly realm in order to become bodhisattvas.

Another bodhisattva, named Avalokitesvara (the Lord Who Looks Down), is worshipped in Tibet and China. Tibetans believe that the Dalai Lama is the reincarnation of Avalokitesvara. The Chinese, on the other hand, consider Avalokitesvara to be a female-shaped deity, and worship her as Guan-yin (One Who Hears the Sound).

Perhaps the most popular bodhisattva in the West is the laughing Buddha (Hoeti), also known as Maitreya. He lives in a paradise called "Tushita" (pleasurable), from where he will return at the end of this age. He will establish "a utopian era in which multitudes will gain enlightenment."[24] In South Asia, many have formed "messianic" cults in the name of Maitreya, proclaiming the arrival of the Buddha era.

"How can a tradition that placed so much emphasis on self-reliance be transformed into a tradition of reliance on a celestial or other worldly savior?" laments a scholar.[25] The answer is surprisingly simple: no religion can survive without a god. The Buddha might have shown us a noble way to live our life, but the problem is that we are humanly incapable of living it. What we really need, therefore, is not another teacher who can theorize the problem of suffering, but a savior who can actually redeem us in the midst of it.

A teacher shows us the way, but a savior becomes the way.

○ ○ ○

In the eyes of Western Buddhism, Jesus is one of the many Buddhas like Siddhartha, the founder of Buddhism. Jesus and Buddha are perhaps the two most compared religious figures in history. They are both revered as embodiments of wisdom and compassion and applauded as great teachers with profound perspectives on the problem of human suffering.

Buddha's solution to the problem of suffering, however, is quite different from that of Jesus. In Buddhism, suffering is unreal; the emotional and physical pain it inflicts on the sufferer is nothing but an illusion. This is not a solution, but an escape from the problem itself.

If confronted with the physical reality of suffering in our day-to-day life, a Buddhist would say that those who "apparently" suffer in the world, according to the law of karma, are suffering because of the bad karma they accumulated from their previous lives. They deserve what they are going through; their misery is of their own making. A Buddhist, therefore, is a detached observer who looks at the suffering world with passive indifference.

In Christianity, on the other hand, God enters the world as an active participant in human suffering. In the physical body of Christ, God experiences the ultimate existential crisis of humanity, and on the cross He embraces the utmost human tragedy. On the cross, God accepts the reality of suffering and makes sure that no one suffers alone in this world. Every occurrence of suffering now has a redemptive meaning because God Himself has gone through suffering before us. Therefore a Christian has the utmost confidence that "all things work together for good."[26]

Jesus, unlike Buddha, did not offer a solution to the problem of suffering. Instead, He became the solution. What He brought to us was not enlightenment of consciousness but redemption of souls. This is the fundamental difference between the Awakened One (Buddha) and the Anointed One (Christ).

As we've seen, the ordinary Buddhist is not looking for a teacher like Buddha, but a savior-like bodhisattva. In the eyes of folk Buddhism, Jesus is one of the many bodhisattvas who came down from the realm of nirvana to the material world. As bodhisattvas exist in both samsara and nirvana at the same time, Jesus is simultaneously present in the life of a believer and at the right hand of the Father. His teachings reflect many Buddhist ideals, and His cross represents the epitome of Buddhist virtues. As an ideal bodhisattva, He will come back again to establish a world in which everyone enjoys enlightenment.

This is perhaps why deep within Buddhism there is an undertone of the Christian notion of "grace." Francis Xavier, an early Roman Catholic missionary to Japan,[27] once described Buddhism as a "Lutheran heresy," because it preached salvation by grace alone, not by human effort.[28]

Japanese Buddhists, for example, believe that Amidaba Buddha will take to Pure Land anyone who chants, "*Namu Amida Butsu*" ("Praise Amida Buddha"). "It was no longer possible to rely on one's own efforts to achieve salvation," said Honen, one of the Buddhist teachers of the medieval era.[29] "The only way to be saved is simply to trust the grace of Amida Buddha."[30]

A bodhisattva can deliver us from this suffering world and lead us into a blissful afterlife reunited with our loved ones. Therefore, taking the bodhisattva vow is an important ritual in Mahayana Buddhism. I remember watching one such ceremony in Los Angeles. A group of initiates from different age groups and ethnic makeups sat cross-legged and close-eyed, repeating after a teacher who officiated the ceremony:

> However innumerable all beings are,
> I vow to save them all.
> However inexhaustible my delusions are,
> I vow to overcome them all.

However immeasurable the teachings are,

I vow to fathom them all.[31]

The Wise Men must have stood at this crossroad, looking for a bodhisattva who can save the world. The road is dark and narrow. But the Star of the Savior is still shining through the cracked roofs of Buddhist monasteries, creating glowing images on the road. They float like lotus petals.

The journey continues.

Chapter 4

THE WORD BECOMES THE LORD

Shabad [Word] is the Guru, upon whom I lovingly
focus my consciousness; ... I am the disciple.
—*Guru Granth Sahib 943–1*

It was four days after 9/11. Balbir Singh Sodhi, an immigrant from
India, walked out of the gas station he owned in Mesa, Arizona. He
was in his traditional Sikh attire: a turban on his head and his long
beard neatly combed and tucked inside it.

A Chevrolet truck drove up to him. A .38 caliber handgun was
put through the window. It spit out five bullets.

The gunman screamed, "All you towel-heads, go home!"

Balbir Singh Sodhi died on the spot. He was the first of the
many Sikh casualties in a series of hate crimes that erupted in
the US in the wake of 9/11. Less than a month later, a group of
teenagers burned down a Sikh temple in New York, claiming it
was named after Osama bin Laden. Another gunman went on a

shooting rampage in a Sikh temple in Wisconsin, killing six people and wounding many others.

Unfortunately, Sikhs, not Muslims, were the unintentional victims in these tragic acts of violence. The perpetrators got them confused with Islamic jihadists because they looked a lot like the terrorists shown on the television screens. Herein lies the sad irony. The religion that persecuted Sikhism the most in the past five centuries of its existence is Islam.[1] But the Sikhs are now victimized for the atrocities allegedly committed by their tormentors.

Sikhism is perhaps the most misunderstood religion. Although it is the fifth-largest religion in the world, with an estimated thirty million followers (double the number of Jews), most research agencies do not attribute "world religion" status to Sikhism. The Sikhs are relegated to the "other" category in most statistics, where they are combined with adherents of Confucianism, Taoism, Shintoism, Jainism, Zoroastrianism, and more.

Sikhism remains largely an ethnic religion based in India, but the diaspora Sikhs have been taking it with them all across the world. It is estimated that there are over one million Sikhs in North America alone. However, they are wrongfully associated with Islam in most parts of the world, primarily on account of their religious attire.

Why would Sikhs follow a dress code that makes them look like Muslims? We need to go back to the origins of their religion to answer this question.

o o o

Sikhism was born in India in the fifteenth century out of a cultural marriage between Hinduism and Islam. Guru Nanak, the founder of Sikhism, was a Hindu who was significantly influenced by the religious worldview of his Muslim teacher.

Nanak was born in Punjab, a region now split between India and Pakistan. He got married at the age of twelve, had two sons, and lived a normal life as a civil servant until he turned thirty. Around this time, he had a profound spiritual encounter while taking a bath in a river. As the story goes, he remained in the river for three days, receiving a series of revelations from God.

The God who appeared to Nanak had no name. Therefore, Nanak called Him *Sat Nam*, or the True Name.[2] The message Sat Nam revealed to him is encapsulated in a single phrase: "There is neither Hindu nor Muslim."

Following this spiritual encounter, Nanak chose to wear an outfit that symbolized this message: half-Muslim (i.e., the turban on the head) and half-Hindu (i.e., the tunic of a Hindu holy man). Even today, all the males "initiated" into the Sikh community follow this dress code, often identified by the "5 Ks":

Kesh: Uncut hair and beard, tucked inside the turban.

Kansha: A comb for grooming the hair and the beard.

Kirpan: A small dagger used for self-defense.

Karha: A bracelet worn on the right hand, like a military dog tag.

Kacha: Long shorts, an undergarment usually worn by soldiers.

Nanak traveled the country preaching the message he received from Sat Nam. He thus became the Guru (teacher) and those who followed him were called the *Sikhs* (disciples).

What Guru Nanak taught is a hybrid religion that evolved out of Hinduism and Islam. Sat Nam, like the Allah of Islam, is a transcendent entity who cannot be described in human terms. The *mul mantra*, the opening verse of the Sikh sacred scripture and a daily prayer of the Sikhs, closely resembles the Islamic confession of faith: "There is but one God. He is True Name, the Creator. He is devoid of fear and enmity. He is unborn, immortal and self-existent. By the grace of Guru He is obtained."

The cosmology of Sikhism, however, finds its roots in Hinduism. A soul transmigrates from one life to the other through different species in the reincarnation cycle. In the end, it receives *mukti*—a blissful union with God (unlike moksha in Hinduism, where we become one with the impersonal Absolute, or nirvana in Buddhism, where we dissolve into emptiness).

This alternate reality, *sachkhand*, is a paradise where we get to reunite with our loved ones while also enjoying the utmost intimacy with God.[3] We enter sachkhand by leading a life of devotion to God, particularly by raising Him through devotional hymns in the sacred scriptures. The loving God gives us grace (*prasad*) to navigate our journey through the different realms of the reincarnation cycle.

o o o

The Golden Temple in Amritsar, Punjab, is an architectural marvel of India, second only to the Taj Mahal. Constructed by Guru Arjan Singh in 1601, this *Gurdwara* (Sikh temple) is considered the religious center of Sikhism.

The memory of my visit to the Golden Temple is colored with its sublime beauty and tranquility. The golden dome, built according to the conventions of Islamic architecture, glittered in the bright sunlight, proclaiming the majesty of God. The towering steeples on the four gates, inspired by Hindu architecture, invited people from all four corners of the world to worship Him.

The first thing I noticed in the Gurdwara was its muted interior. I was surprised to see how simple and plain the sanctuary appeared in contrast to its ostentatious exterior. There were no idols or sacred images, no one performing elaborate rituals or ceremonies. All kinds of idols and religious rituals are prohibited in Sikhism.

The focus of worship in a Gurdwara is the Guru Granth Sahib, the sacred scripture of Sikhism. In order to turn to God, Sikhs believe that one must listen to *gurbani*, the singing of devotional songs from the scripture. It is believed that the repeated reading of the scripture accelerates one's journey to salvation.[4] A typical service consists of devotees singing hymns and presenting their offerings in front of the Guru Granth Sahib.

Sikhism is a religion of Gurus, or teachers. In addition to the founder, Guru Nanak, there have been nine more Gurus in the Sikh lineage.[5] The tenth Guru, Guru Gobind Singh, took the sacred text of Sikhism and designated *it* as the last and the eternal Guru. The Sikhs now revere their scripture as *Guru Granth Sahib*, the Word (or Book) Guru, and treat it as a living person.

A Sikh temple is called *Gurdwara*, "the house of the Guru." The Sikh scripture is written with a sacred script *Gurmukhi*, "the face of the Guru." Sikhism itself can be described as a journey from

our ego-bound world (*manmukh*) to the Guru-bound (*Gurumukh*)
world.

In the Sikh cosmology, the ten Gurus are like ten candles lit by
the same flame. This flame is the Sat Guru, the True Teacher, who
is God Himself. The Sat Guru is the Supreme Light that enlightens
the Gurus, and through them, the rest of the world. As Guru Granth
Sahib puts it:

> My Supreme Guru has created everything.
> I perform devotional worship service to You,
> And fall at Your Feet, O Lord.[6]

The Sat Guru is the creator of the world. He reveals the truth of
God to the world. He is the giver of peace to humanity and is the
only hope of our salvation.[7]

o o o

Geographically speaking, Punjab, the Sikh territory, and Kerala, my
home state, are situated in the northern and the southern borders of
India. I never had the opportunity to befriend a Sikh while I lived in
the country. The first Sikh I ever met was in a church in Canada; she
has since become a good friend and colleague.

Mona was born and raised in an orthodox Sikh family in India.
One day, she attended a Christian youth camp with one of her
friends. She was introduced to the teachings of Jesus, which, at first,
sounded remarkably similar to that of her own religion. After all,

Sikhism encourages its followers to respect all teachers who offer a path to enlightenment.

Mona instinctively knew that the Jesus of the Bible was the historical manifestation of the mythical Sat Guru, spoken of in the Guru Granth Sahib. She also realized that the Sikh Gurus revered Jesus as pure and unique. One such reference is found in Guru Arjan's book, *Sukhmani*, where Jesus is described as someone who "cut off the head of *Rakhshus* [devil]. He is holy and unique Isa [Jesus] of the world.... He is holy and unique and for the whole world."[8]

As Mona continued to study both religions side by side, it seemed to her that "where Sikhism lacked answers, Christianity filled the gaps."

As a musician, she was particularly fascinated by the way in which the language of love and grace, characteristic to Sikh hymns, is reflected in Christian songs. The lyrics of the Guru Granth Sahib express "the devotee's condition: his aspirations and yearning, his agony in separation and his longing to be with the Lord."[9] In the same way, Christianity also portrays the relationship between God and humans in romantic terms, often depicting Christ as a groom and we as His bride.[10]

"Grace is a word that appears in both Christian and Sikh scriptures referring to the undeserved gift of God," posits Mona. "The Sikhs, like Christians, believe in a loving God who gives us grace (*prasad*) in our spiritual journey." The Sikhs, however, do not view grace as the only means to salvation. It is part of God's response to an individual's acts of meditation and charity. In Christianity, grace is an absolute. "There is no other way to receive salvation," says

Mona. "We did nothing to deserve it. I did nothing to deserve it. All that was required of me [to become a Christian] was to respond in faith."

The moment of "enlightenment" Mona had at the youth camp eventually redirected her personal spiritual journey in a completely different direction.[11] Today, she is an ordained minister with the Presbyterian Church of Canada and a noted conference speaker, appearing on numerous stages and in television programs. As I am writing this, she is working on her PhD in theology at one of the most prestigious universities in Canada.

Mona's encounter with Jesus may have been a unique one, but I have since met many Sikhs who share similar sentiments about Him, especially when it comes to His status as an enlightened guru from the perspective of their tradition.

O O O

Who is Jesus according to Sikhism? When the BBC asked this question to a select group of Sikhs, Nikki Singh wrote: "Though I may not see him as one of the Ten Sikh Gurus, he is a distinct and vital parallel who continues to play a very significant role in my life as a Sikh.... Jesus has been a wonderful mirror who in his unique form and vocabulary promoted my self-understanding."[12] This response reveals the respect with which an average Sikh looks at Jesus. They have no difficulty accepting Him as a great moral teacher; some of them may even consider Him on par with the ten gurus of Sikhism.

A Sikh, however, will not equate Jesus (or any of the ten gurus) with the Sat Guru, who is the manifestation of God Himself. Sikhism forbids any portrayal of God in the form of a person. "Let that mouth be burnt, which says that our Lord and Master is subject to birth," says the scripture. "He is not born, and He does not die; He does not come and go in reincarnation."[13] Any individual who has taken birth in this world, including the Sikh Gurus, cannot be considered an incarnation of God.

Having said that, the manner in which Sikhism attributes a personhood to their scriptures, the Guru Granth Sahib, certainly strikes a chord with the Christian doctrine of the incarnate Word. The Guru Granth Sahib, like the Quran, is so revered that any translation from the original Gurumukhi script makes it inauthentic. What intrigues us the most is the name of the scripture itself. The word *sahib* means the "Lord"—a reverential title attributed only to a person. Imagine Christians calling their scripture "Mr. Bible" or Muslims addressing their scripture, "Sir Quran"!

In a Gurdwara, Guru Granth Sahib is "roused" every morning, carried on top of a devotee's head, draped in fine silk, and kept on a throne under a canopy. When it is being read, a whisk is waved over it like a fan, as if to cool it from exhaustion. At the end of the day, it is put to rest in a special chamber covered with ornate blankets. In orthodox Sikh families, Sahib will have "his" own special bedroom like any other member of the family.

Mona recalls how each morning her mother would go into the *Babaji* room, where the Guru Granth Sahib "lived" in their home. "The holy book was on a small table dressed with beautiful silks and brocades. I would sit on the floor in front while my mother conducted the morning ritual of opening the holy book. She would read a passage ... and conclude by saying the *japji*, the Morning Prayer. Every morning began this way and every evening, before sundown, this was repeated when the holy book was closed."

According to Sikhism, God makes Himself known to the world through His *shabad* (Word). The Word is therefore the true Guru. He lives among us to show the way. In fact, He Himself is the way. As Guru Nanak wrote, "The shabad is the Guru, upon whom I lovingly focus my consciousness; I am the disciple."[14]

The Sikh understanding of the living Word finds many parallels in the Christian conception of the Word coming down in human flesh and living among us. When John introduced Jesus to the world, he borrowed a loaded term from the Greek philosophy—*logos*, which is translated "the Word." Word is a tangible expression of the mind; therefore, logos represents the mind of God—a life source that possesses will, intellect, and emotions. In other words, logos is the very essence of God. "In the beginning was the logos," says John. "The logos was with God, and the logos was God."[15]

The logos descended into the human world with a divine mission. His first mission was the creation of the world, where His action was clearly manifested, but His person was hidden. In the next mission, however, we get to see both His action and His person. "The logos became flesh, and dwelt among us," continues John. "And we saw His glory, glory as of the only begotten from the Father, full of grace and truth."[16] The Word became a person.

The world saw the Word in the person of Jesus Christ. The shabad (Word) became the sahib (Lord) in Guru Granth Sahib.

I am beginning to think that the path being lit by the Star of the Savior is not as narrow or singular as I once believed it to be. Was Jesus the Sat Guru that appeared in Nanak's revelation? Did the Wise Men hear his heartbeats pulsating from within the pages of the Guru Granth Sahib—the living Word?

Get closer. Listen with your heart.

Chapter 5

THE MAN WHO BECAME A SIGN

She said: "How shall I have a son, seeing that no man has touched me, and I am not unchaste?" He said: "So (it will be): Thy Lord saith, 'That is easy for Me: and (We wish) to appoint him as a Sign unto men and a mercy from Us.'"
—*Al Quran (Sura 19:20–21)*

The first thing Abdul Rahman did as he entered the dorm was to build a makeshift shrine on his table.

He pulled out a thick, leather-bound book and gently placed it in the shrine. He closed his eyes for a quick second and lowered his head. There was a reverential silence.

It was my second year at the Mahatma Gandhi University in India. Abdul and I were randomly matched as roommates in the college dorm. In the four years that followed, we became close friends and confidants.

The book Abdul placed on the easel was the Quran, the sacred text of Islam.

Despite his worshipful attitude toward the Quran, Abdul rarely read the book. He did not have to. He had memorized most of it, and he could chant many verses on command. He did so in fluent Arabic, with the original intonation.

It took me awhile to realize that Abdul did not know the meaning of these verses that incessantly flowed out of his mouth. Like any other Muslim boy, he had received the formal training to read the Quran in a *madrasa*, the religious school for Muslims. He had to know enough Arabic only to be able to recite the verses; learning the vocabulary was not important. A pious Muslim considers the recitation of the Quranic verses, whether one understands its meaning or not, a noble act in itself. In fact, interpretation of the meaning is a job strictly confined within the domain of the clergy.

It is a foundational belief in Islam that the Quran must exist only in Arabic. The official readings of the Quran are done only in that language. There are no "authorized versions" in other languages, and translation is permitted only if it is accompanied by the original Arabic text. My roommate Abdul's Quran, for example, was in Arabic, but each verse was paired with a translation in Malayalam, our mother tongue. He did not care much for the local language version, because he believed, as many Muslims do, that the very act of translation corrupts the Quran.

Abdul believed that his God, Allah, is the same God as that of the Jews and the Christians. Allah is the one who revealed the Old Testament (*Torah*) to Moses and the New Testament (*Injil*) to Jesus. But the Jews angered Him by killing His prophets, and the

Christians blasphemed His name by making Him part of a "Trinity."[1] Therefore Allah sent the Quran, the uncorrupted revelation, through Muhammad. The Quran, being the latest and the final revelation, supersedes the Jewish Torah and the Christian Injil.

As a truth-seeker, I was intrigued by Abdul's faith and fascinated by his reverence for this sacred text. After much pleading and a lot of persuasion, Abdul allowed me to read his Quran. There was one condition, however: I had to take a shower each time before I touched the book. As unpleasant as it was for any teenager, I yielded grudgingly. In retrospect, I gratefully acknowledge that the enforcement of this rule kept me in good hygiene during my university years.

○ ○ ○

Islam is the second-largest religion in the world, with over 1.6 billion adherents as I write this book.

It is considered a minority religion in India, but the Muslims in India far outnumber the Muslims in Iran, Iraq, and Saudi Arabia combined. Islam is also an integral part of our cultural heritage. Not many people know that the Taj Mahal, the iconic marble mausoleum that has become India's defining cultural icon, is a contribution of Islamic architecture.

As a matter of fact, Islam was born just on the other side of the Arabian Sea that borders India on the west. It happened roughly 1,400 years ago. The Arabian Peninsula at the time was the battleground between two political superpowers—the Byzantine Empire in the West and the Persian Empire in the East. The region was inhabited by various nomadic tribes who had no organized social structure or religion. The only place they came together was at Mecca, a city that is today in Saudi Arabia. Once every year, all the Arab tribes gathered in the same place to offer sacrifices to their gods and goddesses. There were roughly 360 deities housed inside a cube-shaped temple called the *Kaba*, each of them representing the various local tribes and their diverse religious practices.

In the seventh century CE, a prophetic figure appeared on the scene. His name was Muhammad. He claimed that he had a divine mandate to unify the Arab tribes against the invading powers of Byzantine and Persian empires.

Muhammad was neither statesman nor scholar. He was rather an *ammi*, a person with little formal education, and a caravan trader by profession. His parents died soon after he was born.[2] His uncle Abu Talib introduced his young nephew to the caravan business. Muhammad excelled at the trade, and his employer, a widow named Khadija, began to take notice. She fell for his youthful charm and soon decided to marry him. She was forty and he was only twenty-five. The alliance, however, brought Muhammad wealth, social status, and political power.

Over time, Muhammad realized that the real cause of division among the Arabs was not tribal politics, but religion. The best way to unify the people, he believed, was to get rid of all the gods and goddesses (*ilahs*) that separated them, and to bring the nation together under "the God" (*Al ilah*), a name later ascribed to the God of Islam.

Like most prophets who came before him, Muhammad was ridiculed and treated with hostility in his hometown. He was eventually forced to flee to Medina, a city approximately two hundred miles north of Mecca. But in less than ten years, he managed to recruit an army of volunteers in this city and march back to Mecca. After a fierce battle in 630 CE, Muhammad captured Mecca and announced the official founding of Islam.

The root word for Islam (*slm*) in Arabic denotes "submission." A Muslim is someone who has submitted his or her life to the will of Allah. A person can embrace Islam by saying a prayer of confession called *shahada*:

> *lā ilāha illā l-Lāh, Muḥammadur rasūlu l-Lāh.*
> There is no god but Allah,
> Muhammad is the messenger of Allah.

True Muslims follow a common creed, which is often known as the "five pillars" of Islam. They recite the confession of faith (*shahada*); pray five times a day (*salat*); faithfully give a percentage of their earnings to the poor (*zakat*); fast during the month of Ramadan (*sawm*); and aspire to make the ultimate pilgrimage to Mecca (*hajj*), something that each Muslim is recommended to do at least once in a lifetime.

Two years after founding this new religion, Muhammad died unexpectedly, without having named an official successor. A power struggle ensued, out of which two factions emerged. The group that supported Abu Bakr, the father-in-law of the prophet, came to be known as the Sunnis. The group that followed Ali, the son-in-law of the prophet, were known as the Shiites.[3] The rivalry between the factions grew steadily, but when Ali's son Husayn was killed in the Battle of Karbala in 661 CE, the division became irreconcilable.

Though both Sunni and Shia Muslims follow similar doctrines, they keep their distinct Islamic identities, and they consider themselves archenemies.

○ ○ ○

Dudley Woodberry is a professor of Islamic studies at Fuller Theological Seminary in Pasadena, California. Woodberry lived most of his life in Pakistan, soaking in the Islamic culture, and he is highly esteemed in secular as well as theological academia.

"Christians make an inadvertent mistake while they compare the Quran and the Bible," Woodberry tells the students in his class each semester. "A more appropriate comparison would be between the Quran and Jesus."

Students often scratch their heads, trying to make sense of this unlikely connection between a person and a book. But Woodberry's logic is quite simple.

Christians believe that "the Word," an eternal expression of God's mind, took flesh in the person of Jesus Christ. "In the beginning was the Word, and the Word was with God, and the Word was God," wrote the disciple John. "The Word became flesh, and dwelt among us."[4] In Islam, the Word did not become a person; rather, it appeared as a book. The Quran is the miracle creation (*I'jaz Al Quran*) that descended directly from heaven to reveal to us the mind of God.

In Woodberry's language, Jesus Christ is the Word incarnate, but the Quran is the Word "*inlibriate.*"

The marked-up and mutilated Gideon's Bible tucked under my pillow was just as authoritative for me as the Quran was for my friend Abdul. But while Christians consider the Bible to be the "inspired" Word of God, Muslims consider the Quran a "literal" revelation from God.

The Quran is not written by a human author; rather it is a divine revelation that originated from a master book in heaven. Unlike many other sacred texts, it is considered the replica of an eternal "mother book" (*umm-ul-kitab*) that exists in a spiritual realm.[5]

As the story goes, Muhammad had a visitation from angel Gabriel, who revealed to him the words of the mother book. The prophet heard the majestic voice of the angel reverberating in the clefts of Mount Hera:

> Recite in the name of your Lord who created,
> Created man from a clinging substance.
> Recite, and your Lord is the most Generous,
> Who taught by the pen,
> Taught man that which he knew not.[6]

The first word Muhammad heard, "*Iqra*" (Quran: recite), became the title of a series of revelations that he continued to receive until his death. Being an ammi, Muhammad did not write down these revelations meticulously. Instead he memorized them verse by verse and recited them verbatim to his followers. These recitations circulated in the community as oral scriptures until they were later codified and published as one book, the Quran.

The Bible is also a product of direct revelation from God, but it is expressed through the creative minds of a number of different authors and historically conditioned within the context of a community. The power of the Bible, to a Christian, lies in its ability to connect us to the "living Word," who is Jesus Christ.

The Quran is a revelation *from* God, but Jesus is a revelation *of* God.

○ ○ ○

The Quran is the only non-Christian scripture that explicitly talks about the person of Jesus Christ. It refers to him as Isa, the prophet. There are many prophets in the Quran who are also mentioned in the Bible (Adam, Noah, Abraham, Moses, and so on). Jesus is one of those prophets who also received a special revelation (the Injil) from Allah.

The Quran actually paints an illustrious picture of Jesus. He is depicted far more uniquely than any of the other prophets appearing in its pages.[7] Jesus' mother, Mary, is the only woman mentioned by name in the Quran. In fact, an entire chapter, Sura 19, is named after her. Jesus is mentioned fifty-nine times in ninety-two verses, as opposed to Muhammad, who is mentioned (by name) only four times in the Quran.

The Bible does not tell us a lot about Jesus' childhood, except a brief visit to the temple at the age of twelve. But the Quran provides a vivid picture of His infancy, with details that sound outlandish even to Christians. There are stories about the boy Jesus making living birds out of clay and the baby Jesus speaking while He was still in the cradle:[8]

They said, "How can we speak to one who is in the cradle a child?" [Jesus] said, "Indeed, I am the servant of Allah. He has given me the Scripture and made me a prophet. And He has made me blessed wherever I am and has enjoined upon me prayer and zakath as long as I remain alive. And [made me] dutiful to my mother, and He has not made me a wretched tyrant. And peace is on me the day I was born and the day I will die and the day I am raised alive."[9]

The Quran ascribes to Jesus specific titles that imply uniqueness, and even divinity to an extent. For example, it addresses Jesus as the "Word of God" (*Kalimattullah*)—a title that may mean nothing to Muslims, but to Christians, it is loaded with theological connotations. As noted before, in the Bible, "the Word" (logos) does not merely refer to words spoken from the mouth of a prophet or written on the parchment of a sacred text. Logos is a person, an incarnate expression of God's mind. For a Christian, the "Word of God" is a categorical assertion of Jesus' deity and proof of His oneness with God.[10]

The Quran also describes Jesus as the Messiah (the Christ).[11] All prophets can be considered messiahs in the sense that they are anointed by God. But Jesus is called the Messiah (*Al-Masih*), not "a" messiah. The Quran gives the title Al-Masih to Jesus only, just as the Bible attributes the title *ho Christos* (the Christ) to only one person. All prophets, in both the Bible and the Quran, are anointed for specific missions, but there is only one who is "the" Anointed—the One whom the world has been waiting for.

The amazing parallels between the Jesus of Christianity and the Jesus of Islam do not end there. Muslims, like Jews and Christians, believe in a "messianic age," where God is going to destroy the wicked and establish the righteous.[12] In Islam, believe it or not, Jesus is the prophet who is going to spearhead this apocalyptic campaign of Allah.[13] He is considered the climactic figure of human history, who will come back to establish a world in which everybody follows Islam, a life surrendered to God.

Listen to how one of the Hadiths, another authoritative scripture of Islam, describes the second coming of Jesus:

> He will descend (to the earth) . . .
> He will fight for the cause of Islam . . .
> He will break the cross, kill the swine,
> and put an end to war . . .
> He will destroy the Antichrist.[14]

Why is Jesus the only prophet who gets the title "the Messiah"? Why is He the only one who gets to come back to the world? It looks like there is more to the Jesus of the Quran than meets the eye.

o o o

Abdul did not celebrate Christmas. But he believed in the story of Christmas, much more than many Christians who actually celebrated it.

The birth of Jesus, according to the Quran, is a one-of-a-kind miracle. First, the story affirms the "immaculate conception" of Jesus, which means that He was born of a virgin who was kept purified specifically for this very purpose.

Also, the Quranic narrative of Jesus' birth is strikingly similar to that of the Bible, with some added details. In the Quranic version, an exhausted Mary chances upon a stream that appears miraculously in the desert. She drinks water from the stream and gives birth to Jesus under a palm tree.

> So she conceived him, and she withdrew with him to a remote place. And the pains of childbirth drove her to the trunk of a palm tree. She said, "Oh, I wish I had died before this and was in oblivion, forgotten." But he called her from below her, "Do not grieve; your Lord has provided beneath you a stream. And shake toward you the trunk of the palm tree; it will drop upon you ripe, fresh dates. So eat and drink and be contented. And if you see from among humanity anyone, say, 'Indeed, I have vowed to the Most Merciful abstention, so I will not speak today to [any] man.'" Then she brought him to her people, carrying him.[15]

I have come across many Christians who find the miracle of the virgin birth far too difficult to believe. While conservative Christians generally hold the gospel story to be infallible, those in the "progressive" camp view certain elements of it to be allegorical or mythological. The virgin birth is one such area of disagreement. But Islam does not allow scientific rationalism to displace this miracle; it embraces the historicity of Jesus' virgin birth without question.

"How can a Muslim believe Jesus was born without a human father and yet deny the fact that He was more than a mere mortal?" I asked Abdul.

Apparently, I was not the first to pose this question. A group of Christians in Narjan, a city in the southern states of Arabia, once approached Muhammad and raised the same question. At first, the prophet seemed to have no answer. But later, the angel gave him the following revelation:[16] "Indeed, the example of Jesus to Allah is like that of Adam. He created Him from dust; then He said to him, 'Be,' and he was."[17]

Jesus is not the only human being born without a father. God created Adam also without a human progenitor. The virgin birth of Jesus, Muhammad therefore argued, is not a unique miracle with any theological significance.[18]

In my opinion, however, the difference between the creation of Adam and the birth of Jesus is too substantial to compare. For starters, Adam was never born. He was created "as is"—a fully formed adult male, not born of a father or mother.[19] As the first human being, this was the only logical way that he could have been brought into existence. The "birth" of Adam, therefore, was by no means extraordinary; it was the only plausible option for the creation of the first human on earth.

Jesus, on the other hand, could have been brought into the world in a number of different ways. He could have been created from dust like Adam or born naturally like all the other prophets. Yet we read in the Quran that He was birthed by the Holy Spirit, which means the Spirit had to enter a human womb and initiate the natural course of pregnancy and childbirth.[20]

The question now looms large: What was so special about Jesus that prompted God to alter the natural order of procreation and "beget" Him in a virgin's womb? According to both the Quran and the Bible, this was the only time in human history something like this has ever happened. Why didn't God use this specific birthing process for Abraham, Moses, or Muhammad? What was so unique about Jesus that His arrival on the earth had to be engineered in such a special way?

"What if we did a paternity test on Jesus?" I asked Abdul again. "What would we find?"

Jesus' DNA should find a match in Mary as His mother, but what would it reveal about His father? If Jesus was conceived of the Spirit of God without a human father, as the Quran claims Him to be, the paternity test should show, so to speak, God's DNA.

"Who do you think the father of Jesus is?" I rephrased the question.

Abdul hesitated for a moment at my question and then responded with caution. "It has to be God. He created Jesus with His Spirit."

"If God is Jesus' father, why are you offended when I call Him the Son of God?" I asked.

This is where Abdul drew the line. An anthropomorphic representation of God—portraying God with human attributes—is a grievous blasphemy in Islamic tradition. God cannot beget a child without a consort.[21] If Jesus is depicted as the Son of God, it implies that God had sex with Mary to conceive Him.

I tried to explain to Abdul the idea of a theological metaphor. The title "Son of God" is a symbolic term that the Bible uses to describe the divine nature Jesus shares with God.[22] When we describe someone as a "son of a gun," it represents a defining characteristic of the person—that the nature of the man is like that of a gun: volatile, dangerous, and unpredictable—not, of course, that the gun has some kind of claim to his paternity.

When I look at a baby and make a comment such as "she is her father's daughter" or "he is his mother's son," I am actually referring to the unique characteristics the child shares with its father or mother. In the same way, when Christians describe Jesus as the Son of God, they are not talking about God having sex with a mortal woman to produce a human child. What they actually mean is that Jesus exhibits the very attributes only God possesses, and in that sense, He is the most tangible expression of God we have ever seen in this world. In other words, Jesus is the exact representation of God, whom He called His Father.

Abdul was not convinced, but the plot thickens as the Jesus story unfolds in the pages of the Quran. The mysterious beginning of this man is bookended with an even more mysterious ending.

○ ○ ○

Under the snow-covered mountains of Srinagar, a city in the northern part of India, there is a tomb that attracts thousands of visitors every season. A sect of Islam known as "Ahammadiya" claims this to be the tomb of Jesus. In their interpretation of the story of Jesus' crucifixion, He only lost consciousness on the cross. Jesus was buried before His actual death and later revived in the tomb. He then traveled east, all the way to India, where He died an old man.

Orthodox Muslims dispel this story as a fanciful hoax. Even the thought of Jesus' death is an outright blasphemy to a Muslim. The Quran rebukes, and even taunts, Jesus' captors for claiming that they killed Him:

> And [for] their saying, "Indeed, we have killed the Messiah, Jesus, the son of Mary, the messenger of Allah." And they did not kill him, nor did they crucify him; but [another] was made to resemble him to them.... And they did not kill him, for certain.[23]

In the Islamic version of the crucifixion, "the Jews" think that they nailed Jesus to the cross, but it was not Jesus, but a substitute who died in His place. What happened on the cross was nothing but an illusion. God played a trick—it was mass hypnotism of sorts—making the body on the cross resemble (*shubbiha lahum*) that of Jesus.[24]

In one of the many legends circulating in the Islamic world, God made all His disciples look like Jesus at the time of crucifixion. In the end, one of them, most probably Judas Iscariot, ended up getting crucified. In another story, Simon of Cyrene volunteered to die on behalf of Jesus. In yet other stories, the Jewish leaders intentionally killed someone else (most probably one of the guards who arrested Him), because the real Jesus slipped through their hands.[25]

In all these versions, Jesus does not die on the cross. Instead Allah takes Him directly to Himself. "O Jesus, indeed I will take you and raise you to Myself," says Allah. "And purify you from those who disbelieve and make those who follow you [in submission to Allah alone] superior to those who disbelieve until the Day of Resurrection."[26] Jesus now lives in paradise, counting the days until His return to the world as the apocalyptic Messiah.

The death of Jesus, however, is an undeniable historical event. Scholars have successfully retold the story of His life and death using historical records and archeological evidence. An exploration of the quest for historical Jesus is beyond the scope of this chapter, but let me draw your attention to two non-Christian sources, one Jewish and the other Roman.

Flavius Josephus, one of the most noted first-century Jewish historians, writes about Jesus' death in his celebrated book, *Antiquities of the Jews* (93–94 CE): "When Pilate, upon hearing him accused by the men of the highest standing among us, had condemned him to be crucified."[27]

The esteemed Roman historian Tacitus, who wrote elaborately about first-century Rome, describes Jesus' execution by Pontius Pilate in his *Annals of Imperial Rome* (117 CE): "Christus, the founder of the name, had undergone the death penalty in the reign of Tiberius, by sentence of the procurator Pontius Pilate."[28]

The evidence clearly establishes Jesus' crucifixion as a historical reality. The Roman soldiers were well trained to verify the identity of a culprit before they crucified him and then to confirm his death before they buried the corpse. It is very unlikely that the authorities could have been fooled by an illusion or mass hypnotism.

Why, then, would Islam vehemently deny the death of Jesus?

"Allah cannot let an innocent man suffer such injustice. That's why," answered Abdul.

But it is not the first time an innocent man is falsely accused and murdered by the enemies of God, even within the pages of the Quran. Countless prophets have been persecuted and martyred while they were on their God-given missions. Why should Allah be so protective of Jesus?

"He was not like any other prophets," clarified Abdul. "He was not just innocent. He was also pure and holy."

Jesus was more than a prophet. The prophets reminded people of their sins and called them to repentance. But at the same time, they were not immune to the problem of sin. In the Quran, even Muhammad himself was charged with sins against Allah on many occasions.[29]

But Jesus, unlike all other prophets, was destined for a holy life right from His mother's womb. The angel testified that the child Mary was going to carry would be a "faultless boy."[30] The Hadiths report, "No child is born but he is pricked by the Satan and he begins to weep because of the pricking of the Satan except the son of Mary and his mother."[31]

There has never been a perfect man to live in this world, except for Jesus. He cannot be consumed by death like everyone else.

o o o

One of the most festive celebrations I remember from my childhood days was *Bakrid*, the Islamic festival also known as *Eid al-Adha* in most parts of the world. It was also a school holiday, so we would walk around the town greeting people "*Id Mubarak*," and receiving gifts, which usually came in the form of candies. Muslim families also invited us to be part of a great feast that they served on that day.

The Eid feast is prepared from the meat of a goat or a sheep ritually sacrificed (*qurban*) to Allah. The animal symbolizes a lamb, which Abraham sacrificed to God in the place of his son.

The ritual of sacrifice is important in Islam. In another episode in the Quran, God asks Moses to sacrifice an unblemished cow, neither too young nor too old, and yellow in color.[32] This sacrificial animal even has the power to resurrect those who are dead: "So we said: Strike the [dead body] with part of the [sacrificed cow], Allah brings the dead to life, and He shows you His signs so that you may understand."[33]

Although Muslims do not attribute a deeper meaning to the ritual of sacrifice the way the Christians or the Jews do, the Quran seems to suggest otherwise. The passage describing Eid al-Adha is very conclusive in suggesting that Allah "ransomed" Abraham's son with a great sacrifice.[34] How does sacrifice function as a ransom if it does not have a theological significance?

In Christianity, sacrifice serves as a symbol of substitutionary death, where the blood of the animal takes away the sins of the penitent offerer. The animal ransomed for Abraham's son, according to Christianity, foreshadows the Lamb of God that is ransomed for us—Jesus. But in Islam the concept of sin is a bit different. Muslims do not believe in the inherent sinful nature of humanity. Sin is a rebellion against the commandments of Allah. Salvation is, therefore, a matter of obedience and submission to Allah's commandments. There is no necessity for an atonement of any kind.

This is why Islam struggles with the idea of Jesus' death: if Jesus died, it has to reconcile the fact that God did not vindicate this fault-less prophet. Jesus was not just another innocent victim; He was pure and sinless. He therefore could not have been martyred just like any other prophet. God could not have deserted or disowned the only sinless person ever to have lived on this planet. If Allah let Him die on the cross, He would have become a co-conspirator in the most heinous crime committed in human history.

This dilemma takes us to a foundational problem in Islamic theology: "We have in Islam the great anomaly of a religion which rejects the doctrine of sacrifice for sin, whilst its great central feast is a feast of sacrifice."[35] Christianity, on the other hand, makes sense of this paradox by attributing a redemptive meaning to Jesus' death. Jesus was our ransom in a cosmic Eid al-Adha, and His cross the altar of sacrifice in which God accomplished the perfect atonement for the sins of humanity.

Professor Woodberry's words still ring in my ears: "As our eyes drift up to the pinnacle of the mosque, we see a crescent moon—the symbol of Islam. The crescent portrays for us the light Islam reflects and the darkness it contains, the light that recognizes Jesus as prophet and the darkness that does not see Him as priest and king."

○ ○ ○

One quiet Monday morning, my telephone rang unexpectedly. The person on the other end introduced herself as Fatima, a PhD candidate at one of the most prestigious universities in North America.

Her abrupt question took me by surprise: "I am a Muslim. Can I talk to someone about Jesus?"

Fatima had a bizarre story to tell. She had visited an art gallery in Montreal a week before. As she was browsing the paintings, she had chanced upon one in particular—an angry mob getting ready to stone a distraught woman. The woman is begging for mercy. Between the woman and the mob is a man hunched over on the ground. He is scribbling something on the sand with his fingers. The title read: *Casting the First Stone.*

I have seen different renditions of this gospel episode on canvas. But none of them have ever moved me to the extent that Fatima was describing.

"I started crying," said Fatima. "I don't know why. I just wanted to see His face."

Jesus was no stranger to Fatima. She had known Him as one of the many prophets in the Quran. But this was nothing less than a transcendent encounter.

Jesus of the Quran and Jesus of the Bible may intersect in complex and inextricable ways, yet they are far from being identical. One is a prophet who delivered the word of God, and the other incarnate God who came to deliver us. One calls us for obedience to a Master, and the other to a personal relationship with a Father.

My college roommate, Abdul, cringed every time I prayed, "Our Father in heaven." He never thought he could be considered a child of God, and he never dared to address God as "Father." The best Abdul could ever be was His servant; in fact, the name *Abdul* itself is a prefix that means a "servant of."

For a Muslim, religion is more about observing God's law than entering into a relationship with Him. Unlike the God of the Bible, Allah does not express any desire for a personal relationship with His devotees. He is a sovereign judge who demands from us only one thing—strict obedience to His commandments.

"I did not understand the power of forgiveness before I met Jesus," Fatima said to me one day. In the Quran, Allah forgives at His will. But it comes with many strings attached. In the end, one is not really sure whether she is forgiven or not. "That has never made sense to me. It felt unreal. I needed to hear a voice like that woman in the painting did."

Fatima found true forgiveness in the sacrifice of Jesus. Today she considers herself a Christ-follower who happens to be a Muslim.

I have since personally witnessed the Jesus of Islam leading many Muslims to the Jesus of Christianity. As we have already seen, the Quran elevates Jesus to a status high above any other human beings who have ever lived in this world. Although it vehemently denies Jesus' divinity, the depiction of His virgin birth in the Quran undoubtedly points us to the fact that He was more than mere human. A child conceived without a human sperm, by mere logic, should be "superhuman," to say the least.

Jesus of Islam was not just another prophet but a "Spirit from God"[36] who was conceived of the Spirit of God. He lived a sinless life. He performed many miracles, including healing the sick and raising the dead.[37] His life and ministry was so unique that the Quran describes it as "distinguished in this world and the Hereafter and among those brought near [to Allah]."[38] Jesus, therefore, is a "sign unto (all) men," Muslims and Christians alike.

The Wise Men of the East saw the Spirit of God entering the womb of a virgin to conceive a child that would embody the perfection of humanity. Perhaps they knew that the son born of the woman would one day become the Prophet who would reconcile the broken relationship between God and humanity by offering His own life as a sacrifice on the altar of Eid al-Adah. But that would not be the end. As both Islam and Christianity anticipate, He is going to come back again to establish a new kingdom—the domain of God in which everyone leads a life surrendered to His will.

We are waiting for the return of the King.

Chapter 6

THE PIERCED MESSIAH

Then they will look on Me whom they pierced.
Yes, they will mourn for Him as one mourns for
his only son.
—*Zechariah 12:10b NKJV*

It is very unlikely that someone in India would grow up in an environment steeped in Jewish culture. And yet I had that privilege. I went to college in Kochi, a city that was home to one of the country's early Jewish settlements. The Jewish diaspora in Kochi claims its heritage all the way back to the arrival of Israeli traders from the kingdom of Solomon.

"Jew Street" in Kochi is still the hub of business and commerce. One of the major tourist attractions in the city is a synagogue, currently preserved as a national heritage site by the local government. It showcases an amazing display of cultural artifacts: ceramic tiles from China, hand-embroidered rugs from Ethiopia, candelabras from Belgium, and so on.

I used to frequent the Jewish town during my lunch hour in college. I remember buying challah bread from a store painted in the colors of the Israeli flag. It had a seven-branched *menorah*, the Jewish lamp, showcased on the shop window. A Star of David was engraved on its door, and a *mezuzah*, a parchment scroll that contains verses from the *Torah*, the Jewish Scripture, tucked inside the lintels.

As a student, I was fascinated by the history of the Jewish people. I knew that many legendary figures who had changed the course of human history were Jewish—Baruch Spinoza, Sigmund Freud, Albert Einstein, Karl Marx, Steven Spielberg ... and of course, Jesus of Nazareth.

Theoretically speaking, anyone can accept or enter Judaism through a binding ritual of consent, which affirms faith in the covenants God established through Abraham, Moses, and David.[1] But the Jews generally believe that people *inherit* their religion. A person born to Jewish parents is considered a Jew even if he or she does not practice the religion. A non-Jew who believes and observes the Jewish laws, on the other hand, may still be considered a Gentile.

Judaism may be the smallest of all the major religions in the world, but it is the parent religion of two of the largest ones: Christianity and Islam. Indeed, Judaism is much more than a religion. It has inherent connections to race, culture, and national identity. I have often heard people making statements such as, "I am Jewish but not religious." I have also met Jews who confess Jesus as their Messiah and worship Him as God. They describe themselves as "Messianic Jews," not (merely) as Christians.

In college, I had a friend named Solomon. No one knew he was Jewish until he started talking about his family's plan to migrate to Israel. Solomon looked like an Indian, spoke fluent Hindi, and waxed eloquently on Bollywood films. So it came as a big surprise to all of us to find out that he truly belonged somewhere else. Solomon had always dreamed of going to the Promised Land.

The idea of a Promised Land is central to Judaism. The Jewish people believe that the land of Israel is their covenantal right from God. It is considered a mitzvah (a command) to live in Israel. The Jewish people all over the world, including Kochi, conclude their holiday celebrations with a benediction: "Next Year in Jerusalem!"

India once had a thriving Jewish community. At its peak, it claimed to have at least seven synagogues and over two thousand Jews. Today, only a handful of them remain in the country. Most have immigrated to the Promised Land, like my friend Solomon.

Today, as an Indian living in the US, I am also part of a diasporic culture. But I have never felt the same nostalgia Solomon felt for "home." Unlike me, he had been longing for a home that he had never seen.

My home is where my heart is. But Solomon's heart was where his (real) home was.

o o o

Jesus was a Jew. He was raised under the Jewish law, reading the Jewish Scriptures. He attended the Jewish synagogue[2] and faithfully celebrated the Jewish feasts.[3] As Eugene Fisher puts it, "The denial of Jesus' Jewishness is the denial of his humanity."[4]

Many Jewish historians picture Jesus as a political revolutionary of His time. Some consider Him an Essene monk in the light of the

Dead Sea Scrolls, and others an eschatological prophet in the tradition of their apocalyptical literature. But who is Jesus to a Jew today?

Most Jews think of Jesus as a charismatic rabbi who lived in first-century Palestine. The Gospels frequently address Him by this title. There were two Pharisaic schools present at the time, one run by Rabbi Shammai and the other by Rabbi Hillel. The teachings of Jesus resembled closely to those of Hillel, and for this reason, some scholars think Jesus was a rabbi trained at the school of Hillel.

The pattern of Jesus' life fit the life of a rabbi of His time. His teachings were firmly grounded in the Jewish law. He clearly stated that He came "not to destroy the Law, but to fulfill it."[5] Unlike other rabbis, however, He gave new meaning and interpretation to the Law, which became scandalous and blasphemous to many ears. Moreover, He invited Gentiles into a relationship with the Jewish God, which called into question Israel's privileged status as the chosen people of God.

How did an ordinary rabbi become one of the most influential figures in human history? Especially one who was born and raised in a working-class family, lived only thirty-odd years, never went to a formal school, never wrote a book, and was neither a soldier nor a political leader?

Is it possible that Jesus was more than a rabbi or a prophet? First-century Jewish historian Flavius Josephus, while introducing Jesus in his book *Antiquities of the Jews*, wondered, "About this time there lived Jesus, a wise man, if indeed one ought to call him a man."[6] It looks like the contemporaries of Jesus thought of Him as more than mere human. Some Jews even believed He was God in human flesh, and they later came to be known as "Christians."

Of course, it is sacrilegious for Jews to conceive God in human form. "[God] has no semblance of a body nor is He corporeal," says a Jewish prayer.[7] The third of *The Thirteen Principles of Faith* by Moses Maimonides, an early Jewish rabbi, emphatically declares that "the Creator, Blessed is His Name, is not physical and is not affected by physical phenomena, and that there is no comparison whatsoever to Him."[8] In the Jewish worldview, divinity and humanity are mutually exclusive and irreconcilable.

The Jewish Scriptures, however, seem to think otherwise. In the Genesis account of creation, God creates humanity in His "image and likeness." If that is the case, perfect humanity, hypothetically speaking, is a mirror reflection of perfect divinity. The image of God and the image of man, though not the same, need not be mutually exclusive. As paradoxical as it sounds, according to Jewish theology, it is completely logical to believe that a perfect God can express Himself as a perfect man.

We see many accounts in the Scriptures where God presents Himself in human form. When the Lord appears to Abraham, for example, what we actually see is three men approaching Abraham's tent, washing their feet, and eating a meal.[9] In another episode, a mysterious person wrestles with Jacob and dislocates his thigh. We don't know who this man is, but Jacob recollects, "I have seen God face to face."[10]

A few centuries later, a stranger approaches Joshua with a drawn sword in his hands. Joshua immediately falls on his face to the earth and bows down as an act of worship.[11] In the book of Daniel, three Jewish boys are thrown into a blazing furnace. Suddenly a fourth person who looks like "a son of the gods" appears in the middle of the fire.[12]

Theologians describe these events as "theophanies"—human encounters with the divine. Some Christians consider these theophanies to be "Christophanies," or appearances of the pre-incarnate Christ.

The prophets of Israel witnessed God experiencing, and even expressing, human emotions such as anger, love, grief, passion, and hatred.[13] They also recorded a series of esoteric visions in which He would one day enter the world in human form. Isaiah, for example, saw God visiting the earth as a child born of a virgin. It would be the beginning of a new era in which the transcendent God becomes immanent and is called "Immanuel"—God who is with us.[14]

o o o

The Jews are a people in waiting.

Over the last four millennia of their recorded history, they have been subjugated by a number of political superpowers: Egyptians, Babylonians, Persians, Greeks, Romans … the list goes on. Even after becoming an independent nation state a few decades ago, Israel has had no lack of enemies.

Throughout these periodic episodes of oppression, the Jews have been waiting faithfully for a promised savior. God has promised them a deliverer, an eternal king who is going to establish an everlasting kingdom. This promise was an integral part of God's covenant with David:

> I will raise up your descendant after you, who will
> come forth from you, and I will establish his king-
> dom. He shall build a house for My name, and I will
> establish the throne of his kingdom forever.... Your
> house and your kingdom shall endure before Me
> forever; your throne shall be established forever.[15]

The title of this future leader of Israel is "the Messiah." The word *messiah* comes from the verb *m-sh-h* (to anoint), which refers to the anointing ritual for a priest or a king. In that sense, all anointed officials are messiahs. The Scriptures address even Cyrus, a Persian king who helped with the restoration of Israel from Babylonian captivity, as a messiah.[16]

The Messiah, however, is different from *a* messiah. According to the Jewish faith, the Messiah is "a charismatically endowed descendant of David ... raised up by God to break the yoke of the heathen, to reign over the restored kingdom of Israel."[17] He is the iconic savior figure in Jewish theology, who will establish the righteous rule of God in this world.

The prophets envisioned the Messiah to be a mythical hero. "I will raise to David a Branch of righteousness," said Jeremiah. "A King shall reign and prosper, and execute judgment and righteousness in the earth. In His days Judah will be saved, and Israel will dwell safely; now this is His name by which He will be called: The Lord Our Righteousness."[18] Malachi predicted that Elijah would reappear and herald the coming of the Messiah.[19] Another prophet, Zechariah, described in vivid detail the bloody battle that would take place at the Messiah's arrival.[20]

The rabbinic traditions still believe that "the Messianic Redemption will be ushered in by a person, a human leader, a descendant of the kings David and Solomon, who will reinstate the Davidic royal dynasty."[21] The twelfth of *The Thirteen Principles of Faith* reminds the Jews that "though the Messiah delays, one must constantly expect His coming."[22]

In every generation there is an individual, "a scion of the House of David," who has "the potential to be the Messiah."[23] Maimonides postulates a set of criteria for identifying him: if we see a Jewish leader who (a) toils in the study of the Torah and is meticulous about the observance of the mitzvoth, (b) influences the Jews to follow the ways of the Torah, and (c) wages the "battles of G-d"—such a person is the "presumptive Messiah." Based on Maimonides's description, the Messiah will be both a ruler and a teacher.

The history of Israel is riddled with tragic stories of pseudo-messiahs. Today, many Jews downplay the idea of a messianic redemption. Some speculate that the Messiah has already come at some point in history and will not be returning.[24] Others interpret the "*shoah*" (the Holocaust) and the emergence of the state of Israel as "birth pangs of the Messiah," who is about to come.[25]

As a Christian, I am taught to believe that Jesus was the Jewish Messiah. My Bible has a comparison chart that shows how different events in Jesus' life fulfilled the messianic prophecies of the Hebrew Scriptures. The Hebrew Scriptures have given us different elements of His résumé. We know the Messiah's gender (male), His family (Judah), and even the city in which He was to be born (Bethlehem).[26] Obviously, Jesus fits the profile.

My Jewish friends find such comparisons far-fetched and even downright offensive. "The messianic prophecies are not fulfilled until and unless the Jewish nation triumphs over the world," says one of my rabbi friends from Toronto. The Messiah will reestablish the political sovereignty of Israel. He will rebuild the Holy Temple in Jerusalem. All exiles will return to the Promised Land, including the "ten lost tribes." There will be universal disarmament and worldwide peace, and the whole world will come to acknowledge and serve the Jewish God.[27] Obviously Jesus has failed to accomplish all of these important messianic tasks, at least while He was here on earth.

So, the Jews are still waiting for their Messiah.

O O O

Superman, the iconic action hero from the cartoon world, is known as the Man of Steel all over Metropolis. Only a few people are aware of the fact that the clumsy reporter at the *Daily Planet*, Clark Kent, is his alter ego. We cannot pick between Clark Kent and Superman. They are one.

The Messiah is the Superman of the Jewish Scriptures. He is the transcendent hero who is going to fly in from outer space to save the world at the time of apocalypse. But on occasions, the same Scriptures also record cryptic visions of this superhero's alter ego.

"And I will pour on the house of David and on the inhabitants of Jerusalem the Spirit of grace and supplication; then they will look on Me whom they pierced," cries out Zechariah. "Yes, they will mourn for Him as one mourns for his only son, and grieve for Him as one grieves for a firstborn."[28]

A pierced Messiah? It is a dramatically different picture from the one the Jews have in mind. A suffering hero does not match the criteria they have set for the promised savior. But this alter ego keeps appearing in the visions of the prophets. Isaiah, for example, sees the picture of a bruised and battered Messiah and describes Him in vivid detail:[29]

> He has no stately form or majesty
> That we should look upon Him,
> Nor appearance that we should be attracted to Him.
> He was despised and forsaken of men,
> A man of sorrows and acquainted with grief;
> And like one from whom men hide their face
> He was despised, and we did not esteem Him.
> Surely our griefs He Himself bore,
> And our sorrows He carried;
> Yet we ourselves esteemed Him stricken,
> Smitten of God, and afflicted.
> But He was pierced through for our transgressions,
> He was crushed for our iniquities;
> The chastening for our well-being fell upon Him,
> And by His scourging we are healed.
> All of us like sheep have gone astray,
> Each of us has turned to his own way;
> But the LORD has caused the iniquity of us all
> To fall on Him.[30]

Jewish scholars struggle to reconcile these conflicting pictures of their savior—the triumphant superhero and His suffering alter ego. A number of them believe that there could be two distinct Messiahs instead of the one God had originally promised.

"The dilemma was solved by splitting the person of the Messiah in two," says Raphael Patai, a Jewish scholar. "One of them, called Messiah ben Joseph, was to raise the armies of Israel against their enemies, and after many victories and miracles, would fall victim to Gog and Magog. The other, Messiah ben David, will come after him, and will lead Israel to the ultimate victory, the triumph, and the Messianic era of bliss."[31] According to this theory, Messiah ben David (son of David) is the superhero and Messiah ben Joseph (son of Joseph) is his alter ego.[32]

In certain Talmudic writings, Messiah ben Joseph is resurrected after his death in the battle between the kingdoms of Gog and Magog:

> And when he will see that Messiah ben Joseph will be slain, he will say before Him: "Master of the World! I ask nothing of you except life!" God will say to him: "Even before you said, 'life,' your father David prophesied about you as it is written, He asked life of thee, Thou gavest it him."[33]

This "double identity" of the Messiah is a baffling concept for Jewish scholars. But the New Testament Scriptures propose a solution—what if both of these messianic figures converged in one person?

According to Christian theology, Jesus of Nazareth, the Jewish rabbi from first-century Palestine, is both a suffering servant and a sovereign king.

"It did not take much time for me to realize that both these portrayals of the Messiah are pointing to one savior figure," says Sharon, a Messianic Jew I met in Los Angeles. "He will lead his people to the ultimate victory over evil in the future (as the son of David), while vicariously identifying with their pain, suffering, and even death (as the son of Joseph) at the present."

Jesus came to this world as the son of Joseph once, and He will be coming back again as the son of David. The entire world, including the Jewish people, will look upon the One "whom they have pierced," and realize that he was indeed the promised Savior.[34]

The Messiah, for the time being, is hiding in plain sight.

o o o

As of this writing, I have never attended a Passover meal. The closest I have come to it so far is the Seder meal some churches put together during Easter week. But my Jewish friends consider this mock-Passover celebration a misguided attempt to mimic a religious ritual rightfully belonging only to them.

Passover (*Pesach*) commemorates an event in the history of Israel in which the angel of death "passed over" the Jewish homes, sparing the lives of their firstborn sons. In memory of this incident, the Jewish families are instructed to celebrate Pesach on the tenth day of the first month of the year by slaughtering a lamb and eating its meat with unleavened bread.[35] The blood of the lamb is to be daubed on the doorpost and lintels of their homes.

The New Testament claims that Jesus was the Passover lamb sacrificed once for all.[36] "This is My body which is given for you," said Jesus, attributing a new meaning to the Passover meal. "This is My blood of the covenant, which is poured out for many for forgiveness of sins."[37]

It is interesting to note that in the original Passover meal, one had to take the blood of the lamb and sprinkle it, first on the top lintel of the front door and then on the two side posts. In doing so, they inadvertently formed a sign of the cross, the ultimate sacrifice represented by the Passover lamb.

Sacrifice brings reconciliation between God and the sinner, thus moving humanity closer to God. The Hebrew term for sacrifice originates from the word *korban*, which literally means, "to come close."[38] The priestly codes in Leviticus prescribe the blood of an animal also as a requirement for the atonement of sins. The act of sacrifice denotes a process of substitution, where the offered animal is enduring the punishment the offerer rightfully deserves.

The symbolism of atonement is portrayed even more vividly in the festival of *Yom Kippur* (the Day of Atonement).[39] On the day of this festival, two goats are sacrificed for the redemption of the entire nation. Historically, the first goat was killed for the sins of the children of Israel, and its blood was sprinkled on the Mercy Seat in the Holy of Holies, the innermost sanctum of the temple. The second goat would be released into the wilderness after the high priest transferred the sins of the nation symbolically upon its head. This goat would wander in the wilderness, bearing the sins of the people, and was eventually eaten by wild beasts.

Today, because there is no temple, the Jews believe that *teshuvah* (penitence) is the only thing that is necessary for atonement. "At the present times when the Temple no longer exists, and we have no altar for atonement, nothing is left but teshuvah," says Maimonides. "Teshuvah atones for all transgressions."[40]

However, according to *Mishna* (the codified oral traditions of Judaism), teshuvah atones for minor sins only, and "if a serious sin has been committed it hangs in suspense until Yom Kippur comes and atones."[41] In other words, repentance is an integral part of the sacrifice, but it is not enough on its own to atone for sins.

The animal sacrifices we see in the Hebrew Scriptures, according to Christian theology, are a foreshadowing of the ultimate atoning sacrifice of Jesus Christ.[42] As the blood of a lamb covers the sins of the Jewish people, so the blood of a sinless Messiah cleanses the whole world from its sins. Jesus' sacrifice on the cross thus fulfills the symbolic sacrifices in the Hebrew Scriptures. He identifies with both sacrificial lambs of Yom Kippur—the lamb that was "slain from the foundation of the world," and "the Lamb of God who takes away the sin of the world."[43]

o o o

When we read the Hebrew Scriptures through the Christian lens, Jesus emerges as the actualization of the covenant symbols of Judaism and the personification of God's eternal promise to the Jewish people. He is the Messiah who once came into the world as a suffering servant, but He is going to come back as the triumphant king to reclaim the Promised Land—the kingdom of God.

The Jewish people may not see Jesus as their Messiah yet, but today they appreciate the fact that He stood in solidarity with the moral principles of the Torah and therefore "relationship between Jews and Christians will not weaken Jewish practice."[44]

In 2015, a group of prominent Orthodox rabbis issued a joint statement titled, *To Do the Will of Our Father in Heaven: Toward a Partnership between Jews and Christians*,[45] in which Christianity is described as "the willed divine outcome and gift to the nations."

"Jesus brought a double goodness to the world," say the rabbis. "On the one hand he strengthened the Torah of Moses majestically," and on the other hand, "he removed idols from the nations," instilling them "firmly with moral traits." They applaud Christians for their work for the sake of the kingdom of God and promise that their "reward will not be denied."

In the same vein, *Nostra Aetate* (*In Our Age: Declaration of the Relationship of the Church to Non-Christian Religions*), a document issued by the Catholic Church, affirms that the Jewish covenantal bond with God still remains valid despite the arrival of Christianity.

"Although the Church is the new people of God, the Jews should not be presented as rejected or accursed by God, as if this followed from the Holy Scriptures," says *Nostra Aetate*. "All should see to it, then, that in catechetical work or in the preaching of the word of God they do not teach anything that does not conform to the truth of the Gospel and the spirit of Christ."[46] The Catholic Church also affirms the fact that the cross of Christ has reconciled both the Jews and the Gentiles to God, making them part of one family.

In Protestant circles, esteemed Christian theologians such as Jürgen Moltmann view Christianity as an extension of the Jewish mission to the world, in anticipation of the "*eschaton*"—the end of this earth—awaited by both traditions.[47] Christianity does not supersede Judaism; it rather universalizes the Jewish religion. The salvation of Israel will come when the full measure of Gentiles is brought into Christ.[48]

Although the Jews do not see Jesus the way the Christians do, they have shepherded the tradition heralding His coming from time immemorial up until the present day. They have persisted through centuries of persecution, and they continue to wait in hope for the Messiah, both in Israel and in all of the countries to which they have been scattered.

There are still a few Jews remaining in Kochi. Although no one gathers at the synagogue anymore, they continue to make their presence felt in the religious landscape of my college town. Each time I visit Kochi, I take a drive through the Jewish town. I utter a silent prayer for the Jews all over the world, reflecting on what Leo Tolstoy once said: "He who has been for so long the guardian of prophecy, and who transmitted it to the rest of the world, such a nation cannot be destroyed. The Jew is everlasting as is eternity itself."[49]

In the treasure chest of prophecy the Jews so carefully guarded, the Wise Men found God's best gift to humanity. The Star of the Savior that guided them is still lingering on the horizon, illuminating the prophetic visions of a universal Messiah.

We are almost there.

Chapter 7

THE EMPTIED GOD

> Christ Jesus, who, although He existed in the form
> of God, did not regard equality with God a thing
> to be grasped, but emptied Himself.... Being found
> in appearance as a man, He humbled Himself by
> becoming obedient to the point of death, even
> death on a cross.
> —*Philippians 2:5b–8*

I am an avid fan of Bono, the lead singer of the legendary band U2. I admire not only what he does, but also who he is. What captivates me the most is not his musical talent (impressive as it is) but his uncanny ability to frame complex theological insights into everyday language. Listen to the following comments he once made to an interviewer:

> Christ says: No. I'm not saying I'm a teacher. Don't
> call me teacher. I'm not saying I'm a prophet. I'm
> saying: "I'm the Messiah." I'm saying: "I am God

incarnate." ... So what you're left with is: either
Christ was who He said He was—the Messiah—
or a complete nutcase. This man was strapping
himself to a bomb, and had "King of the Jews" on
his head, and, as they were putting him up on the
Cross, was going: OK, martyrdom, here we go.
Bring on the pain![1]

As absurd as it sounds, I am amused by his rendering of C. S.
Lewis' famous "trilemma theory" with such simplicity and levity.[2] If
Jesus is not Lord, He is either a liar or a lunatic. If He is not God,
He is either bad or mad. If Christ is not worthy of worship, He is
worthy of no respect.

Jesus is a paradox, much like a rock star who preaches theology
in the mosh pit.

"Who do people say that the Son of Man is?" Jesus asked His
disciples once.[3]

He often described Himself by that title—the "Son of Man,"
a term in contemporary language that may sound something like
"Average Joe."[4] That's appropriate.

Jesus was not born a prince like Buddha; neither was He a war-
rior like Muhammad. Statistically speaking, His life seemed just as
insignificant as the lives of most of us on this planet. He was born
into a working-class family in an obscure village, and He lived most
of His life as a blue-collar construction worker. He did not have
formal education, and most of His acquaintances were uncultured
country folks or social misfits—fishermen, tax collectors, prostitutes,
and the like.

The founder of the largest religion in the world was truly an average Joe.

His disciples couldn't help but notice, however, that there was something special about their Master. Unlike the other teachers who speculated on abstract theories, He spoke about absolute truths with clarity and authority. He performed signs and wonders in front of their eyes. More importantly, they were told that His mother conceived Him without any human contact. If that is the case, He must have been something more than just another man.

Some of the bizarre statements Jesus made about Himself also stood out in their minds. A group of Jews were once bragging about how proud they were of their patriarch Abraham. Jesus looked them straight in the eyes and said, "Before Abraham was born, I am."[5]

What He said sounded wrong on so many levels. It was grammatically incorrect to begin with. Instead of using the verb "I was" in past tense, Jesus said "I am," which happened to be a title reserved exclusively for God in the Jewish tradition. When God revealed Himself to Moses in a burning bush a few centuries before, He introduced Himself, "I am who I am."[6]

It was no secret that Jesus addressed the God of Moses as His "Father." Jesus also claimed that He came from heaven to do the will of His Father, and that He was going back to His Father's house where He had built many "mansions" for His followers. But when His followers asked who this Father was, He made another outrageous comment: "He who has seen Me has seen the Father."[7]

They scratched their heads. How could the Father and the Son be the same person? Had Jesus made a mistake?

"I and the Father are one," reiterated Jesus.[8]

This was a shocking—even blasphemous—claim. And yet it was not what Jesus said that amazed His disciples the most; some of what He did also appeared outlandish.

One day, a group of friends brought a paralytic man to Jesus. They knew Jesus was going to heal him, of course. But just before healing him, Jesus did something unimaginable: He said that the sins of the paralytic man were forgiven.

How could He do such a thing? Healing was one thing. But forgiving someone's sins was a prerogative exclusively within the purview of God. Not even the high priest had the authority to absolve sins. How then could a wandering teacher, who did not even belong to the priestly tribe, do so?

"Why does this Man speak blasphemies like this?" people murmured. "Who can forgive sins but God alone?"[9] The disciples might have suspected at that point that the words and actions of their Master were bordering on the levels of insanity.

Bono and C. S. Lewis express the same concern using different vocabularies. Jesus can't be just another great teacher or prophet. He must have been a manipulative deceiver or an eccentric blockhead. That is, unless He is, as Peter, one of His disciples, put it …

"The Christ, the Son of the living God."

○ ○ ○

The Son of God?

I hope Peter did not say it too loudly. It could have easily gotten him arrested for treason—even killed, for that matter. There was only one person who could have been addressed as the "Son of God"—the Roman emperor himself.

Everyone knew that the Romans considered their ruler to be God in human flesh. If Peter had taken a closer look at one of the coins in his pocket, he would have noted the inscription *Divi Filius* (Son of the Divine One) embossed on it. Julius Caesar was called the son of Zeus. Augustus Caesar was introduced as "son of a god, who shall restore the golden age and spread his empire."[10]

The title "Son of God" was reserved exclusively for the emperor. It symbolized power, authority, and divinity. It was not a random title that could be ascribed to anyone, let alone a penniless preacher from a remote village in Palestine.

But to our surprise, Jesus did not correct Peter. We know He admonished Peter on many occasions for blurting out such infelicitous comments. But this was not one of them. "Blessed are you, Simon Barjona," said Jesus, "because flesh and blood did not reveal this to you, but My Father who is in heaven."[11] Instead of rebuking Peter, Jesus chose to applaud him. He described this discovery as some sort of divine revelation.

Authentic religion, this passage suggests, has to be a product of personal discovery through God's revealing work. Peter had one such personal revelation here, and Jesus celebrated that. But Jesus then instructed the disciples not to reveal this truth to anyone. The discovery of Jesus' true identity is a matter of individual revelation, something outside the realm of mind and reason.

Christianity is a spiritual journey on the path of a progressive revelation. It starts with the knowledge of Jesus as the Son of Man, but it advances toward the realization of Him as the Son of God.

Peter was well ahead of the curve in this journey. Another disciple, John, progressed even further. He got to "see" Jesus as He truly is— beyond this temporal world, in His heavenly glory. In the maddening loneliness of a solitary confinement on the island of Patmos, years after Jesus had been taken back up to heaven, the Son of God appeared to John. This is how he describes this nearly indescribable event:

> In the middle of the lampstands I saw one like a son of man, clothed in a robe reaching to the feet, and girded across His chest with a golden sash. His head and His hair were white like white wool, like snow; and His eyes were like a flame of fire. His feet were like burnished bronze, when it has been made to glow in a furnace, and His voice was like the sound of many waters. In His right hand He held seven stars, and out of His mouth came a sharp two-edged sword; and His face was like the sun shining in its strength. When I saw Him, I fell at His feet like a dead man. And He placed His right hand on me, saying, "Do not be afraid; I am the first and the last, and the living One; and I was dead, and behold, I am alive forevermore, and I have the keys of death and of Hades.[12]

Jesus is just as divine as He was human. Although He appeared in the body of the son of man, His true essence is that of the Son of God.

o o o

How can a person be perfectly human and perfectly divine at the same time? It sounds like an oxymoron. Perhaps Jesus was a demi-god, 50 percent man and 50 percent God?

Historically speaking, Jesus was born and raised in a modest Jewish family in the first century in Palestine. But Christians (and also, as we have seen, Muslims) believe that His mother was still a virgin when He was conceived in her womb. He grew up as a normal child by all accounts, but the process of His birth was far from what can be considered "normal."

We don't know much about Jesus' life until He turned thirty or so. This is when we see Him again, now as an itinerant preacher proclaiming the arrival of "the kingdom of God," a spiritual domain in which God rules as King.

Jesus' teaching was self-authenticating. It was its own authority. But the political leaders of the time charged Him with insurrection. Ironically, the man who was born a peasant was executed with a sign that read "King of the Jews" nailed to His cross and a crown (of thorns) upon His head.

But in this story, death was only the beginning. On the third day after His burial, Jesus came back to life. His resurrection, Christians claim, is proof of a cosmic victory He won against the kingdom of darkness. His final triumph is yet to come, however. Christians (and Muslims) are eagerly waiting for His "second coming," when He is going to establish the kingdom of God for all eternity.

Jesus, in His death and resurrection, showed Himself to be both true God and true man. But His "hybrid identity" was always a controversial and disputed topic. Indeed, the question of how to understand Jesus' simultaneous human and divine natures sharply divided Christians in the first few centuries following His ascension.

In the third century, a faction known as the Arians, the disciples of Bishop Arius, believed that Jesus was neither fully God nor fully man. He was rather an in-between being, a lesser god or a higher man. God created Him in the beginning, the Arians claimed, and then appointed Him to fashion the rest of the creation. He was later assigned to save humanity from their sins, for which He will be rewarded with sovereign authority over the world.

"That is preposterous!" said another group, called Monophysites. "He was fully divine and only appeared to be human." The Monophysites believed that Jesus' body was made of celestial substances, which created an illusion of flesh and blood. He was never born, lived, or died; what the people saw was nothing but an apparition. Jesus of Nazareth (the son of man) was an illusion created by the Cosmic Christ (the Son of God).

"You mean God tricked us with a phantom?" scoffed the Nestorians, followers of Bishop Nestorius. For them, Jesus' humanity was the most important reality. Jesus was first and foremost an ideal man who lived an exemplary life, which stands as a perfect model for all of humanity to follow. His divinity ensued as a result of His perfect life; it was something that enveloped His humanity like a halo. God invaded the body of Jesus of Nazareth so that He—God—could experience true humanity. The divinity of Christ possessed the humanity of Jesus to accomplish a specific mission.

Another group, called Adoptionists, took the middle ground. Jesus was an ordinary human for the first thirty years of His life, they speculated. But at the time of His baptism, God adopted Him as His son. The son of man suddenly became the Son of God. But then God abandoned Him on the cross. His divine nature evaporated, and the human nature was restored while He suffered and died. On the cross, the Son of God became the son of man once again.

These disputes on the true identity of Jesus tore the church apart into deeply divided factions. For centuries, church fathers desperately tried to articulate how human and divine elements coexisted in Jesus' being:

- "He alone is both God and man, and the source of all our good things," wrote Clement of Alexandria.[13]
- "The origins of both his substances display him as man and as God," argued Tertullian. "From the one, born, and from the other, not born."[14]
- Origen declared, "Although he was God, he took flesh; and having been made man, he remained what he was: God."[15]

Though the arguments were nuanced, the implications were profound, because each group accused the others of heresy and blindness to the true nature of Christ.

The schism continued in the church until the Council of Nicaea in 325 CE declared Jesus as "God of God, Light of Light, very God of very God … being of one substance with the Father."[16] With this claim, the church was affirming that Jesus was both fully human and fully divine—that His divinity was identical to that of the God whom He called "the Father."

The Council of Chalcedon (451 CE) expanded upon this, proposing the "hypostatic" union between God and Jesus, in which "the human and divine natures of the Person of Christ co-exist, yet each remains distinct."[17] The Athanasian Creed likewise affirmed, "Though he is God and Man, yet he is one Christ, not two, and he became man not by changing his deity to humanity, but by blending humanity with deity."[18] In other words, the identity of Jesus is a fusion of perfect humanity and perfect divinity.

We have already established that Jesus is called the "Son" but not in the sense that He is created by the Father. It is rather a theological metaphor that may seem complex to us but that would have made perfect sense to His immediate audience.

When people of first-century Palestine addressed Caesar as the Son of God, they did not mean that Zeus birthed Caesar. Instead, what they meant was that Zeus and Caesar were one and the same being. The emperor was just as divine as he was human. In the same way, when Christians address Jesus as the Son, it does not mean that He was birthed by the Father or that He is in any way inferior to the Father. Instead, it affirms that both God and Jesus are one and the same being.

This is why the New Testament writers are very intentional in describing Jesus as the *begotten* Son of God.[19] "To beget is to become the father of; to create is to make," explains C. S. Lewis. "And the difference is this. When you beget, you beget something of the same kind as yourself.... What God begets is God. Just as what man begets is man. What God creates is not God. Just as what man makes is not man."[20]

We are all sons and daughters of God in the sense that we are created by Him. But only Jesus is begotten of God. Only He shares God's DNA.

Jesus, in other words, is 100 percent human and 100 percent divine. But how does this math make sense?

○ ○ ○

The prophet Isaiah once had a spectacular vision of God, not unlike the one John, the disciple of Jesus, had of the Son of God. Isaiah saw God sitting on a lofty throne, with the train of His robe flowing through the temple court. The foundations of the temple shook as six-winged seraphim shouted His praises: "Holy! Holy! Holy!"[21]

Roughly six hundred years later, John retells this story in his gospel, but with an interesting twist.[22] In order to emphasize people's stubborn refusal to believe in Jesus, John quotes one of Isaiah's prophecies: "He has blinded their eyes and He hardened their heart, so that they would not see with their eyes and perceive with their heart."[23] This verse is picked straight from the scene of Isaiah's majestic vision. But the next statement John makes is even more interesting: "These things Isaiah said because he saw His glory, and he spoke of Him"—*Him* here referring to Jesus.

We know that the One who was featured in Isaiah's vision is none other than God Himself. But in John's account, it was Jesus who appeared to Isaiah. The writer of the gospel is looking at the same person the prophet had seen six centuries previously.

In another episode in the Bible, Moses waits behind a rock to see God with his naked eyes.[24] No one can look at the face of God and remain alive, but Moses gets to see God's "back" through a cleft in the rock. He interacts with this God on many occasions and even receives a handwritten tablet from Him. Yet the writer of the book of Hebrews says that Moses considered "the reproach of Christ [Jesus] greater riches than the treasures of Egypt."[25]

Moses lived almost fourteen centuries prior to the arrival of Christ. How could he bear the reproach of Christ? Was Christ the same being as the "I am who I am" that Moses had been serving faithfully throughout his life? Was the God Moses saw through the cleft of the rock actually Jesus Himself?

It is quite audacious to suggest that the Hebrew God Yahweh and the Christian God Jesus are one and the same. But it is precisely what these passages seem to do. John and the writer of the book of Hebrews are referring to the same entity that Isaiah and Moses wrote about in their respective books.

This is the reason Christians believe in the idea of a triune God—One who has three identities (*hypostases*) in one substance (*ousia*). The One God exists in three consubstantial persons: the Father, the Son (Jesus Christ), and the Holy Spirit.

In the Trinitarian framework there is no logical disparity in assuming that the God who appeared to Moses, Isaiah, and other Hebrew saints was the same God who walked with Peter, John, and the other disciples in first-century Palestine. They are simply different personifications of the same triune God.

o o o

But if Jesus is God, why wouldn't He say it plainly? Why would He want to keep us guessing?

In order to answer this question, we need to understand the subversive nature of Jesus' mission. He was in the process of founding an "upside-down" religion where the earthly standards are reversed: the first will be last and the last will be first; whoever saves his life will lose it and whoever loses his life will gain it. He envisioned an inverted kingdom that is "not of this world." The King of this secret domain will not walk around giving out His business cards to everyone; only His true subjects will recognize Him. As I mentioned before, religion has to be a personal discovery.

On the other hand, it is also not true to say that Jesus never made public claim of His divinity. As we have already seen, He asserted on many occasions that He and the Father are one and that whoever has seen Him has already seen the Father. His immediate audience recognized the avowal of equality with God in His voice, and they took up stones to throw at Him. "You, being a man, make Yourself out to be God," they cried out.[26] Jesus may not have shouted from the rooftop that He was God, but the clues He left for those who wanted to discover His divinity were not by any means subtle.

Jesus also displayed divine attributes only God would have possessed. The disciples affirmed on multiple occasions, "You know all things," clearly recognizing His omniscience.[27] John recollects, "Jesus knew from the beginning who they were who did not believe, and who it was that would betray Him."[28]

He demonstrated His omnipresence in the healing of those who were physically at distant locations. Where two or three are gathered together in His name, He claimed, He would be "in their midst."[29]

His omnipotence is manifested in the many miracles He performed, which included even raising a corpse four days after its burial. Jesus claimed in no uncertain terms: "All authority has been given to Me in heaven and on earth."[30]

We also have many witnesses in the Scriptures who would gladly testify to His divinity:

Angels worshipped Jesus: "When He again brings the firstborn into the world, He says, 'And let all the angels of God worship Him'" (Hebrews 1:6).

The devil "bowed down" before Jesus, revealing His true identity as the Son of God: "Seeing Jesus from a distance, he ran up and bowed down before Him; and shouting with a loud voice, he said, 'What business do we have with each other, Jesus, Son of the Most High God? I implore You by God, do not torment me!'" (Mark 5:6–7).

Prophets described Jesus as the mighty God and eternal Father: "For a child will be born to us, a son will be given to us; and the government will rest on His shoulders; and His name will be called Wonderful Counselor, Mighty God, Eternal Father, Prince of Peace" (Isaiah 9:6).

The disciples worshipped Him, and addressed him as Lord and God: "And those who were in the boat worshiped Him" (Matthew 14:33). "And they came up and took hold of His feet and worshiped Him" (Matthew 28:9). "When they saw Him, they worshiped Him" (Matthew 28:17). "And they, after worshiping Him, returned to Jerusalem with great joy" (Luke 24:52). "Thomas answered and said to Him, 'My Lord and my God!'" (John 20:28).

The others who were outside the disciples' band also recognized His divinity and worshipped Him: "After coming into the house [the magi] saw the Child with Mary His mother; and they fell to the ground and worshiped Him" (Matthew 2:11). "And [the man born blind] said, 'Lord, I believe.' And he worshiped Him" (John 9:38).

We know that only God is worthy of worship. If Jesus is considered worthy of worship by the angels, the devil, the disciples, and everyone else, then His divinity requires no further proof.

According to the Scriptures, Jesus is "God … manifested in the flesh," who is "the King eternal" and "the only God." He is also "the image of the invisible God" and "the exact representation of His nature." In Christ, "all the fullness of Deity dwells in bodily form."[31] Paul addresses Him as the "great God," John describes Him as "the true God," and Peter portrays Him as "our God and Savior."[32]

The verdict is loud and clear: Jesus of Nazareth is the personification of the almighty God, the most tangible expression of divinity we can ever aspire to witness. In Him, the transcendent God has become immanent, to whom we can relate as to another human being.

In Christ, God ended religion and began a relationship.

O O O

C. S. Lewis was once asked what is the one thing that makes Christianity stand apart from the rest of the religions.

"Grace," said Lewis. Only in Christianity is salvation offered as an act of God's grace, not as a reward of human merit. We are not judged based on what we do but on who we are in Christ. That is the difference between the transcendent God of world religions and the immanent God who became Christ.

Religions operate on the assumption that human actions are weighed on a moral scale and rewarded accordingly in the afterlife. In Eastern religions, if your bad deeds outweigh your good deeds, you will go levels down in the reincarnation cycle. In Abrahamic religions, if your sinful deeds surpass your virtuous deeds, you will be doomed to hell. Religious life thus becomes a complex game of "snakes and ladders" with unexpected twists and turns, not to mention an even more unpredictable outcome.

In Christianity, on the other hand, God takes the burden of karma upon Himself and suffers the moral consequence of human actions. When the law of karma tyrannically demands "do this" or "do that," Jesus triumphantly declares on the cross, "It is done!"

In Christianity, righteousness is not about doing the right thing, but it is about having the right relationship with God. Jesus has established a new relationship between God and humanity through His atoning death, according to which the primary criterion for judgment is not what we do, but who we are to God. We are not doing right things in order to become righteous, but because we are righteous. This is how the radical theology of grace in the gospel upends the law of karma in world religions.

When Jesus said, "Peace I leave with you; My peace I give to you,"[33] He did not mean "peace" in a clichéd sense, as often used by politicians and pageant queens. The peace that Jesus offers is not "as the world [religions] give," but it is a cosmic assurance that comes from the realization that our relationship with God is no longer defined by the checks and balances of karma but by the extravagance of grace He has lavished upon us on the cross. This is why the Christian gospel is called the Good News.

The Good News, unlike the messages of other religions, is not about the transcendent reality of God. The Good News proclaims the truth of God becoming Christ. "For God so loved the world" that He chose to give us neither law nor philosophy, but Himself.

The Christian message, therefore, is not merely a truth claim; it is Truth personified. The gospel is a person—a living, breathing entity.

Jesus Christ was not a "messenger" of God like Moses or Muhammad were; He was the message.

"Who is this man?" asks Bono. "Was He who He said He was, or was He just a religious nut?"[34]

I too have wrestled with this question. Jesus made me choose between the extreme ends. There was no middle ground. Either He was the image of the invisible God or He was a disillusioned religious freak.

So here we are. Exactly where we started: with a paradox. Christ *is* a paradox. He is both human and divine at the same time. The Christian message is a paradox: "For whoever wishes to save his life will lose it; but whoever loses his life for My sake will find it." And the Christian life is a paradox: "When I am weak, then I am strong."[35]

Of course, when the infinite God invades the realm of the finite, it is bound to end up in a paradox. Sylvia Dunstan, an alumnus of my seminary at the University of Toronto, sat down to ponder this paradox, and penned these beautiful verses to one of my favorite hymns:

> You, Lord, are both lamb and shepherd,
> You, Lord, are both prince and slave,

You, peacemaker and sword-bringer,

Of the way you took and gave.

…

Worthy your defeat and victory.

Worthy still your peace and strife.

You, the everlasting instant;

You, who are our death and life.[36]

Jesus is a mystery, as God Himself is. A mystery cannot be explained but it can certainly be explored and experienced. Perhaps the best way to explore a paradox is to experience it for oneself.

It is the first and the foremost lesson I learned from the Wise Men. They embarked on an adventurous expedition from the East to the West in search of the greatest mystery ever revealed to humankind. The long and arduous journey brought them to a ramshackle barn in an isolated corner of the world. There they discovered, tucked inside a heap of straw, clinging to the bare chest of a woman—an emptied God, the ultimate paradox!

Chapter 8

THE TRUE MYTH

The story of Christ is simply a true myth: a myth
working on us in the same way as the others, but
with the tremendous difference that it really happened.... In Christ whatever is true in all religions
is consummated and perfected.[1]

—*C. S. Lewis*

We have been following the footsteps of the Wise Men on an
incredible journey through countries, cultures, and religions. In
this spiritual pilgrimage from the East to the West, we came across
many "Christ figures" who bear close resemblance to the Jesus of
the Bible.

In the Hindu pantheon, we encountered the avatar, an embodied god with a salvific mission. In the Buddhist universe, we met
the bodhisattva, an enlightened teacher who has taken the vow to
rescue humanity from a suffering world. In Sikhism, we witnessed
God revealing Himself to the world through the personification of
His Word. We came face to face with the Jesus of Islam, the only

human ever to have entered the world without a father and the only prophet who is going to come back again to reestablish God's domain on the earth. We explored the Jewish texts that struggle to reconcile the conflicting portrayals of the Messiah as a triumphant king and as a suffering servant.

God's redemptive plan for the world has been unfolding in every culture and in every religion since the beginning of time. Isn't it incredible!

We are now at a crossroads. We have two possible hypotheses to explain the presence of these Christ figures in world religions, each leading to dramatically different conclusions.

The first hypothesis is termed the "Christ myth theory," according to which early Christians fabricated the Jesus story, or at least doctored it, based on various pagan myths already available in other cultures. Jesus was not a historical figure, this theory says, but a cosmic symbol that represents every man and woman. His life symbolizes the divine and human natures God has infused in all of us. This "Cosmic Christ" resides in our humanity, waiting to be actualized into divinity.

This theory has been debated and debunked countless times, yet it remains a favorite among the New Age gurus and pulp fiction authors. In my own research, I find the quasi-scientific methodologies of the Christ myth theorists to be speculative at best, and their arguments ambiguous and unconvincing.

For example, they blame Christians for stealing a fictional savior figure from Middle Eastern mythologies but fail to show how exactly such a nefarious scheme was orchestrated by a group of powerless and persecuted people in the first century. The theory also tries to disprove the existence of the historical Jesus, but historians seldom doubt the fact that a man named Jesus existed two thousand years ago, even if they are skeptical of His divinity.

The second hypothesis is that God has done this intentionally. It is a missional theory that suggests that God has implanted a version of the Christ myth in every religion and culture with the goal of preparing the world for the arrival of the real Christ in the fullness of time. In other words, God revealed His plan of redemption to the whole world in symbolic forms, which would one day point them to the real Redeemer—Jesus of Nazareth, in whom all Christ figures find their historical fulfillment.

C. S. Lewis, for example, argued that the person of Christ does not stand in opposition to the heroes of pagan mythology but is the historical culmination of what these myths were foreshadowing. "We must not be nervous about 'parallels' and 'pagan christs,'" claimed Lewis. "They ought to be there."[2] Christianity, according to him, is a "true myth"—a cosmic story that became a historical reality.

The sublime pictures of the redeeming savior we found in other religions might be secret codes God has programmed into their sacred narratives in order to prepare them for the arrival of His Son. Therefore, Lewis says, "in Christ whatever is true in all religions is consummated and perfected."[3]

The Jesus story in the Gospels is not a rehashed version of ancient mythologies, but the historical manifestation of the primordial truths God has engraved in every religion and in every culture.

o o o

Don Richardson, a missionary from Canada, traveled to Indonesia in the early 1960s with his wife and their six-month-old child. Their mission was to preach the gospel to the indigenous Sawi tribe of West Papua.

There was one problem, however: the Sawi were cannibalistic headhunters of the jungle who preyed on anyone who came across their path.

When they disembarked the boat and stepped onto the island, the Richardsons probably thought their story might end right there. But surprisingly, the Sawi people extended them a warm welcome. It is not uncommon for cannibals to use trickery and deception to befriend their victims. Was this reception part of one such devious scheme?

It turned out that the Sawi genuinely accepted the Richardsons into their community. It was an unexpected turn of events, and it took awhile for them to figure out why their fate changed so dramatically.

When they entered the village with an infant child in their hands, the Richardsons were unknowingly becoming part of a tribal ritual—one that symbolized friendship and peace in the Sawi community.

Whenever battles broke out between two Sawi villages, a man from one village would walk over to the enemy territory carrying his son in his hands and present him as an offering of peace. If the village chose to adopt the child and raise him as one of their own, there would be reconciliation between both parties. The child thus became a symbol of peace in the midst of war and was named "the peace child."

As they learned of this tradition, the Richardsons were struck by its parallel to the gospel narrative. In order to restore the broken relationship between God and humanity, God walks into the enemy territory with His only Son as a peace offering. Isn't the story of the peace child, they wondered, an allegory of the Jesus story?

Jesus is our Peace Child. If we accept Him, there will be peace and reconciliation between us and God.

The Richardsons used the peace child as an analogy to communicate the gospel to the Sawis. The rest is history. Today, there is a thriving Christian community in West Papua, which continues to cherish the eternal peace they found in the ultimate Peace Child.

After this episode, Don Richardson unearthed many other clues God has placed in different cultures that point people to His salvific plan for the world. He calls these "redemptive analogies" and says they are "aspects of a people's own culture, which contribute to the redemption of that people."[4]

I have discovered such redemptive analogies not only in the sacred texts of world religions but also in more popular forms of cultural narratives, such as film and literature. In a university class on film criticism, I came across the idea of the "Christ figure" in film. This is an "allegory [that] follows the main thread of the Christ story, while disguising it through a surface narrative.... The figure is strong enough to exist by itself, but points to a meaning far beyond this existence for its ultimate truth."[5]

Christ figures in a story are characters whose lives parallel the Christ story in some aspects, exhibiting the fundamental nature of Christ's redemptive work. They need not always be religious characters themselves, yet they draw on the "universal cultural symbolic value of the Jesus persona."

A Christ figure in film can be disguised as women, clowns, or even as animals.[6] Two readily recognizable Christ figures are John Coffey in *Green Mile* (1999) and Babette in *Babette's Feast* (1987). John Coffey is an innocent prisoner on death row, convicted of a crime he did not commit. He heals the sick, awakens the dead, and even shares Jesus Christ's initials. Babette, like Jesus, is the epitome of sacrificial giving that gives until the giver becomes exhausted and extinguished.

There are many films that feature redemptive narratives with a Christ archetype: *The Passion of Joan of Arc* (1928), *Bicycle Thieves* (1948), *Shane* (1953), *One Flew Over the Cuckoo's Nest* (1975), and *Shawshank Redemption* (1994) are commonly cited examples.

A Christ figure in film and literature is a mythical archetype embedded in its narrative arc. Scholars have long observed patterns of thoughts instinctual to all humanity, which influence and even shape our cultural narratives—be it philosophy, art, or religion. Carl Jung, one of the founding fathers of modern psychology, called them "archetypes of the collective unconscious."[7] Jung argued that there are "primordial images" embedded in the human psyche, which manifest themselves as archetypal characters in cultural myths across the world.

It is precisely this insight that Joseph Campbell applied to comparative mythology, that Stan Lee applied to superhero comics, and that George Lucas applied to the *Star Wars* anthology. Christ figures that appear in our cultural narratives, therefore, can be considered products of the subconscious theological memory of the culture.

What if the Christ figures we observe in film, literature, and the sacred narratives of world religions are a mythical archetype God has embedded into our collective unconscious as a precursor of the coming Savior?

If that is the case, we can see how Christ could have been present even outside the traditional boundaries of Christian religion, like the unknown god of Greek mythology or of the Rig Veda. The promise of salvation woven into the sacred texts of world religions, as C. S. Lewis argued, may have finally found its fulfillment in the person of Jesus Christ.

It is important to remember that the unknown God is not the Christ of the Bible, nor is He the Cosmic Christ of the New Age spirituality that transcends all cultures and religions. He is rather a Christ figure—a type, or symbol, that has the potential to function as a pointer to the Christ of the Bible. He is one of the mythical archetypes God has implanted in our religious consciousness to prepare us for His ultimate self-disclosure in Christ.

o o o

The theological stance we have discussed so far can be framed within the biblical pattern of God's revelation to humankind. According to the Scriptures, there are two separate streams of revelation: *general revelation,* through which God makes His presence felt in the universe, and *particular revelation,* where God makes His salvific plan for the world known in Jesus Christ. General revelation is available to anyone with a seeking mind and a listening heart, but particular revelation comes only through the providential grace of God.

Let us picture God as the proverbial "man upstairs" in the attic. He exists in a reality above our material world, separated by an impassable ceiling. But suppose He chooses to make a crack in the ceiling and lets His glory shine into the world. As the light of His revelation falls from the attic to the floor, it dissipates through the air at varying levels of intensity.

GENERAL REVELATION

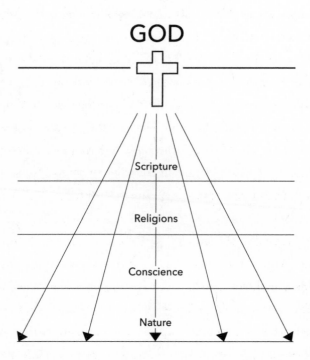

The highest level of revelation available to humanity today, according to Christianity, is the Scripture. The Bible is "God-breathed" (*theopneustos*), and therefore it is both infallible and inerrant.[8] It is called "the Word of God" because it is the best expression of God's mind in written form. Through the Bible we receive the clearest and the most intimate picture of who God is and what He desires in the world.

But at the lowest level, God makes Himself known to the world through His fingerprints ingrained in the created universe. "The heavens are telling of the glory of God; and their expanse is declaring the work of His hands," sings the psalmist.[9] The beauty of nature and the wonders of creation invoke the presence of God in human spirit. Although God remains largely invisible to the material world, "He did not leave Himself without witness." He manifests His benevolence by providing "rains from heaven and fruitful seasons, satisfying [our] hearts with food and gladness."[10]

In the next level up, the light of general revelation is reflected in our conscience. When we confront a moral choice, for example, an "inner voice" prompts us to a particular direction, often against our own self-interest. When we do something wrong, we are haunted by a "guilty conscience," and when we make it right, we enjoy a "clear conscience." The conscience thus becomes our moral compass, functioning as God's law "written in [our] hearts."[11] In the absence of an absolute written law, it allows us to become "a law to [ourselves]" by providing an inherent ability to discern between right and wrong.[12]

One level up, God's revelation is manifested in the many religions of the world, most of which possess at least a partial understanding of the one true God, as we have seen. Religions are essentially products of the human search for God, and their sacred writings emerge from our insatiable quest for ultimate truth. Therefore, it is natural to assume that all religions possess the power to produce genuine spiritual experiences at varying intensities.

The Roman Catholic Church was quick to observe and appreciate the light of God's revelation in other religious traditions. "The Catholic Church rejects nothing that is true and holy in these religions," says *Nostra Aetate*. "She regards with sincere reverence those ways of conduct and of life, those precepts and teachings which, though differing in many aspects from the ones she holds and sets forth, nonetheless often reflect a ray of that Truth which enlightens all men." It is important to note, however, that the centrality of Jesus Christ is of paramount importance to the Catholic creed. Jesus is the one "in whom men may find the fullness of religious life, in whom God has reconciled all things to Himself."[13]

Today even conservative theologians in the evangelical spectrum recognize and acknowledge the presence of God's redemptive revelations in other religions. Amos Yong, a leading voice in the fields of theology and missiology, goes so far as to argue that the Holy Spirit is at work in other religions, and for this reason, "the religions of the world, like everything else that exists, are providentially sustained by the Spirit of God for divine purposes."[14] Such a belief does not drag us down into universalistic pluralism; it only recognizes the activity of God's Spirit in unexpected places.

God's general revelation filters through multiple lenses of different focal lengths—in nature, in human conscience, and in world religions, and even more brightly in the Bible. Each level projects different images of God—big, small, stretched, or skewed. But in the end, each tier of revelation reflects only part of the fullness of God. His ultimate "self-disclosure" happens at the attic ceiling, in Jesus Christ, who is "the image of the invisible God."[15]

God might have cast the shadows of His salvific plan in the sacred writings of world religions. But in Jesus Christ, these shadows turn to light, and God draws the whole world into the source of light itself.

○ ○ ○

If all religions contain traces of God's revelation, then what, one might wonder, is the relevance of Christianity in a multicultural mosaic? If redemptive grace can be found in other religions, why did Jesus ask us to go across the world and preach the gospel?

It is important to remember, in the attic analogy, that each religion frames God's revelation through its own theological filter. In this process, the true revelation gets skewed and corrupted. Paul says that in the foolishness of their wisdom, people abrogate the infinite God into finite forms, thus becoming "futile in their speculations." As a result, they can see the source of revelation only through broken and dusty glasses.

The kernels of general revelation available in world religions can grant us only an *awareness* of God; but the Good News that Christianity presents to the world is His *nearness*. While religions point to a transcendent deity, the gospel invites us to an immanent One—"Immanuel," the God who is with us!

Different religions claim to provide different ways to God. But only Christianity introduces a way *from* Him. "I have come down from heaven," said Jesus.[16] No religious leader has ever dared to make such an audacious claim. The teachers and prophets of other religions promise to take us to places they themselves have never been. Only Jesus can lead us into the presence of God—because that is exactly where He came from. Only the One who descended from God can help us ascend to Him.

The Bible makes it very clear that there is only one way to God, and that way is Jesus. "No one comes to the Father but through Me,"[17] Jesus stated unequivocally. "There is salvation in no one else," asserted Peter even more fiercely. "For there is no other name under heaven that has been given among men by which we must be saved."[18]

It's clear that Jesus is the only way to God … but does the Bible say there is only one way to *Jesus*?

There are over forty-five thousand Christian denominations in the world, most of them claiming to be exclusive ways to approach the one Jesus.[19] In the same way, what if there is another way—or ways—to Jesus that we are unaware of?

Read it carefully. We are not saying that there is more than one way to God. If we were, we would certainly be contradicting the Bible. But if we say there could be more than one way to Jesus, we might only be challenging a loosely held church dogma, not the Bible itself. It is possible that there exist people who are in communion with Christ without ever being in the community of His disciples, like the young man we met in the gospel story,[20] who followed Jesus without following His followers.

What if Jesus stands at the intersection between God and world religions, perfecting God's plan of redemption as the many ways *to* God meet the only way *from* Him?

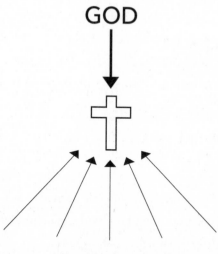

ONLY WAY

GOD

CHRIST FIGURES

Make no mistake: we are not talking about universal salvation, nor do we condone a worldview in which everything is subjective and relative. As a Christian, I strongly believe that any religion that does not recognize God's self-disclosure in Christ, no matter how honest and benevolent it might be, cannot function as a direct path to God.

The theory of general revelation, however, provides us a path to affirm our Christian conviction that Jesus Christ is the only way to God while paying due respect to people of other religious beliefs and worldview assumptions. It also helps us articulate the uniqueness and significance of the Christian faith in a pluralist world with deserving appreciation toward the wide spectrum of spiritual experiences entwined in its cultural tapestry.

We build this theory on the framework provided by "fulfill-ment theology,"[21] according to which there are genuine allusions to the arrival of Christ in other religious traditions. Apart from the historical revelation unfolded through the prophets of Israel, God had been slowly unraveling a mystical revelation through the sages and seers of various cultures. Both these streams of revelation culminate in God's ultimate self-disclosure in the person of Jesus Christ.

From the perspective of fulfillment theology, a pre-Christian religion is like the moon that radiates the light of the sun, which is yet to rise in the horizon. The moonlight guides us in our spiritual darkness, for which we should indeed be grateful, but in reality, we have been guided by the reflection of the sunlight all along. Christ, the true source of light, has now risen, inviting us to the fullness of the Supreme Light.

○ ○ ○

Jesus came into this world to, among other things, prove that God is not a racist.

In Him, the many faces of the Christ figures we observed in different religions crystallized and manifested in history. The grace of God that brings salvation appeared to "*all* men."[22] It is the "good news of great joy," meant for "*all* the people."[23]

This is the lesson I learned from the Wise Men. The Savior's birth was for the East and the West. He established His kingdom for the Jews and the Gentiles. God does not play favorites. There is a broad spectrum of inclusivity within the exclusivity of His gospel.

When I am sharing the gospel with my neighbors of other faiths, therefore, I am not selling them a new religion; I am only introducing them to a person who embodies the fullness of their own religious expectations.

While in seminary, I heard Karl Barth, arguably the most brilliant theologian of the twentieth century, pondering on "God's strange voice outside the walls of Christianity."[24] Barth believed that Christ's death was intended for all men, and He could indeed reconcile all the world to the Father if He chose to do so. "I do not preach universal salvation," Barth insisted. "What I say is that I cannot exclude the possibility that God would save all men at the Judgment."[25]

In the same vein, Karl Rahner, an eminent Catholic theologian, suggested that people could be saved by the salvific work of Jesus Christ even though they have never had an opportunity to know Him personally or acknowledge their faith in Him publicly. Rahner described them as "anonymous Christians"—Christians outside the Christian tradition.[26]

C. S. Lewis followed suit: "If you are a Christian you do not have to believe that all other religions are simply wrong all through," said Lewis. "There are other people who are being led by God's secret influence ... who thus belong to Christ without knowing it."[27]

All these ideas sounded like borderline heresy at the time. Were Barth and Rahner preaching a politically correct gospel where everyone reaches the same destination irrespective of the paths they have chosen? Did Lewis believe that all religions are essentially one and the same? Of course not! They were simply contemplating the possibility of people following Jesus without being consciously aware of the fact that they are following Him.

We believe that the Old Testament saints received salvation through Jesus Christ though they had never seen nor heard Him. They did so by believing in the Christ figures hidden in the Hebrew Scriptures. Is it then possible that God would extend the same grace to my ancestors from India who have never heard the name "Jesus" or "Christ," through no fault of their own? What if their faith in the unknown God of Rig Veda helped them discover Jesus, like the Wise Men of the East, even through unorthodox ways? What Good News that would be!

Jesus told the Jews that He did "not come to abolish but to fulfill"[28] their law. If He were born in India, would He have said the same thing to the Hindus? I don't know. According to fulfillment theology, the Christ event took place as a fulfillment to the promise of prophetic predictions of all preexisting Christian sources, not just the Hebrew Scriptures. We can make a case that Hinduism has more in common with Christianity than Judaism based on the amazing parallels between the Christian story and Gita's conception of avatar or the Vedic notion of sacrifice. More importantly, the idea of incarnation—God's self-emptying process—a doctrine that is central to the Christian theory of atonement, is revealed more clearly in the Hindu sacred texts than in the Old Testament. In that sense one can even argue that Hinduism was more preparatory for the arrival of Christ than Judaism!

In the end, there is one thing we know for sure: God has put eternity in our hearts,[29] regardless of our ethnic, cultural, or religious differences. There is a built-in, intuitive, religious instinct common to all of us—a collective religious consciousness—that induces a genuine quest for God in the depth of our being. Jesus Christ is the ultimate fulfillment of this quest of humanity.

Remember that boy in the blue shirt? Now I feel like I am with him on the stage, becoming part of God's unfolding magic act in this world. I look around to see "the others," watching us from the dark. I cannot see them, but I know they are there, and they play an important role in this act even though they do not realize it yet. When the Magician takes a bow, all the lights in this cosmic theater will turn on, and the hidden witnesses will be revealed.

Once, the resurrected Jesus walked with two travelers on the road to Emmaus. He did not, in that moment, look like the Jesus they knew, nor did He sound like Him. They did not recognize Jesus because "their eyes were prevented from recognizing Him."[30] But when the time came, "their eyes were opened and they recognized Him."[31]

One day, this grand unveiling will happen in front of the blinded eyes of humanity. God will remove the "shroud that enfolds all peoples, the sheet that covers all nations."[32] The whole world will see the apotheosis of the fragmented revelations that already exist in our midst, converging in the fullness of Jesus Christ. Until then, all we can do is to continue exploring these stories—the stories of the unknown followers of the unknown God.

In the book of Revelation, we see Jesus knocking at the door of a human heart. The one who opens the door will dine with Him.[33] As I read this passage, I cannot help but imagine a group of neighbors across the street, watching this man who is standing at my door. They see Jesus from different vantage points, perceiving

His image in dramatically different ways. But the one who opens the door will get to experience Him for who He truly is.

What if Christ, standing at my door, is visible to my neighbors of other faiths through the windows of their own religious traditions? What if God has allowed world religions to capture blurred visions of the same Jesus who revealed Himself fully and more tangibly in the Christian faith?

If you are someone who has already opened the door to Jesus, I hope my stories help you notice those who are trying to catch a glimpse of Him through the windows across the street. If you are one of those neighbors peering through the windows, I invite you to come to the door.

Open it wide and see who He truly is!

EPILOGUE

My twelve-year-old self curls up inside the blanket, still listening to the Vedic chants seeping in through the bedroom window.

The Gayatri mantra has come to an end. The temple priest is now chanting another versatile prayer in lyrical Sanskrit:

> *Asatho ma Satgamaya*
> (Lead me from Delusion to Truth)
> *Thamaso ma Jyothrigamaya*
> (Lead me from Darkness to Light)
> *Mruthyor ma Amrutham Gamaya*[1]
> (Lead me from Death to Life)

The cone-shaped loudspeaker on top of the church dome responds almost instantly:

> I am the Truth (John 14:6)
> I am the Light (John 8:12)
> I am the Life (John 14:6)

A profound prayer receives a providential answer.

The Supreme Light trickles in through the window, embracing me with its invisible arms. Its warmth and tenderness are comforting.

The Star that guided the Wise Men is still moving through the darkened sky beyond the horizon. Its shimmering rays radiate the "true Light which … enlightens every man."[2]

I am waking up.

NOTES

Prologue

1. John 1:4–5 KJV.

2. John 1:9 KJV.

3. John 9:5.

Chapter 1: Following the Star

1. Miller, P. (1988). "Kerala: Jewel of India's Malabar Coast," *National Geographic*, May.

2. Deuteronomy 14:2 NIV.

3. The city of Cochin—more details about the Jewish connection of Cochin in chapter 6.

4. Genesis 12:2.

5. The Bible acknowledges that this was partially true. See Genesis 12; 20.

6. Genesis 12:18–19.

7. Genesis 12:3b.

8. The magi are considered to be kings in their land.

9. W.J., M. (1809). *The Lusiad or The Discovery of India*. London, Allen and Co. Page 240.

10. "According to Western church tradition, Balthasar is often represented as a king of Arabia, Melchior as a king of Persia, and Caspar as a king of India." *Encyclopedia Britannica Online*, s. v. "Magi," accessed May 24, 2016, www.britannica.com/topic/Magi.

11. Genesis 9:16.

12. Isaiah 49:6 NIV.

13. Isaiah 56:7 NIV.

14. See Isaiah 19:19–25.

15. Amos 9:7.

16. Kaiser, W. C. (2012). *Mission in the Old Testament: Israel as a Light to the Nations*. Grand Rapids, Baker Academic. Page 32.

17. Jonah 4:11.

18. The northern kingdom of Israel was destroyed by Assyrians in 722 BCE.

19. 2 Chronicles 35:21.

20. 2 Chronicles 35:22.

21. Genesis 14:18–20.

22. One hypothesis suggests that both El and Elyon were Canaanite names for Yahweh Himself.

23. Psalm 110:4.

24. Exodus 18:1–27.

25. 2 Chronicles 2.

26. Isaiah 45:1.

27. Mark 9:38–40; Luke 9:49–50.

28. Mark 9:39–40.

29. John 10:16.

30. See Acts 10.

31. 2 Peter 3:9.

32. Romans 10:12–13.

33. 1 Timothy 4:10.

34. Acts 17:30.

35. 1 Timothy 2:4.

36. Isaiah 42:6 NKJV.

37. Matthew 5:14.

38. Acts 17:28 NKJV.

39. Encyclopedia Britannica, Macropeadia, 15th ed., vol. 3, p. 924.

40. Another excerpt from this poem, "Cretans, always liars," is also quoted by Paul in Titus 1:12. The "lie" of the Cretans was that Zeus was mortal; Epimenides considered Zeus immortal.

41. Acts 17:22–34.

42. Paul certainly knew the story behind the unknown God. He quotes Epimenides' poem not only in his sermon, but also later in his epistle to Titus (Titus 1:12) As a matter of fact, he addresses Epimenides not as a poet, but as a prophet. According to legends, it is Epimenides who initiated the cult of the unknown God.

43. See Acts 17:22–34.

44. Rig Veda X:121, www.sacred-texts.com/hin/sbe32/sbe3215.htm.

Chapter 2: The Descent of God

1. Of the TV show *The Mindy Project* (NBC/Fox 2012–2015), among other acting credits.

2. Satya Nadella (CEO, Microsoft), Sundar Pichai (CEO, Google).

3. Miller, L. (2009). "We are all Hindus Now." *Newsweek*. August 31, 2009.

4. "I'm a Hindu: Julia Roberts." *Times of India*. August 7, 2010. Retrieved November 20, 2016, from http://timesofindia.indiatimes.com /entertainment/english/hollywood/news/Im-a-Hindu-Julia -Roberts/articleshow/6265252.cms.

5. Gita 7:21–22.

6. Rig Veda 1.164. 46.

7. Vivekananda, S. (1989). *The Complete Works of Swami Vivekananda Almora*. Advaita Ashrama. Page 19.

8. Gita 6:1.

9. Gandhi is a classic example of a Karma yogi. His political struggle was not pursuit of power, but he called it *Satyagrha*, which means "the quest for truth." There was always a spiritual undertone to all his outward actions.

10. Chandogya Upanishad VI.8.7.

11. Brihad Aranyaka Upanishad I.4.10.

12. Rig Veda 10.81.3.

13. Gita 18:65–66, www.holy-bhagavad-gita.org/chapter/18. (Compare it with Matthew 11:28: "Come to Me, all who are weary and heavy-laden.")

14. Gita 11:44.

15. His identity is not as static as the God of the Bible; in fact, Bhakti yoga believes that all personal deities are nothing more than Iswara representing himself in different forms. A devotee is free to choose from among many gods appearing in the *puranas*, the collection of Indian mythologies.

16. Mahabharata Book 3. CCLXX page 531 (SacredText.com).

17. Brahma is the creator god with four heads that face all different directions. He is not worshipped by Hindus. Shiva is the lord of dance (*nata raja*) who sets the rhythm of the world. The world will end when he stops dancing. He often appears with his consort goddess Shakti, also a manifestation of the mother goddess. Vishnu sleeps over a cosmic ocean on a great serpent made up of the remains of the previous universe. His consort goddess: Lakshmi (fortune). Those who worship Shiva are called Shivites, and those who worship Vishnu are Vaishnavites.

18. When I wrote this, his film *Avatar* (2009) was the highest grossing film with a reported revenue of over $2.7 billion. It has since been eclipsed by *Avengers: Endgame*.

19. (1) Fish/*matsya*, which saved the world and Vedic texts from a primordial flood; (2) Tortoise/*korma*, which helped with churning the ocean for *amrurtham* by supporting the mount on its back; (3) Boar/*varaha*, which brought back the earth that was sinking to hell (*patal lok*) to its original position; (4) man-lion/*narasimha*, who saved his devotee Prahlada from the murder plot devised by his own furious father; (5) dwarf/*vamana*, who tricked king Mahabali to give up his kingdom; (6) Parasurama, who destroyed the enemies of the Brahmins, using a big axe; (7) Rama, a dutiful husband and king who fought a 1,000-headed demon to save his wife Sita; (8) Krishna, the charioteer who played a pivotal role in Kurukhestra Yudha; (9) Balarama, older brother of Krishna, a war hero who taught both sides of the warring faction the art of war but remained neutral in the war; and (10) Kalkin, an avatar to appear at the end of his ear. Not all avatars are full manifestations of his godhead. There are the *nitya avatara*, the continual presence of god in the world (through the lives of saints and sages), the *amsha avatara,* a temporary disguise god uses to accomplish a specific task at a specific point in time, and the *poorna avatara,* the only perfect manifestation of god, who *is* Lord Krishna (or Lord Rama in another tradition).

20. Nathan, R. S., Ed. (1983). *Symbolism in Hinduism*. Bombay, Central Chinmaya Mission Trust. Page 116. Rama is Dharma (duty)-oriented, whereas Krishna is Karma (action)-oriented.

21. Chinmayananda, S. (1983). Radha and Krishna. *Symbolism in Hinduism*. R. S. Nathan. Bombay, Central Chinmaya Mission Trust. Page 112.

22. Jeremiah 31:20; John 3:29; 2 Corinthians 11:2; Revelation 19:7.

23. Bhagavata Purana 2.7.38.

24. Revelation 21:1–5.

25. Schouten, P. J. (2008). *Jesus as Guru: The Image of Christ Among Hindus and Christians in India*. Amsterdam, Rodopi.

26. Kurup, A. M. (1977). "The Sociology of Onam." *Indian Anthropologist*. Vol. 7. No. 2. Pages 95–110. JSTOR, https://www.jstor.org/stable /41919319?seq=1.

27. Sarbatoare, O. "Yanja – Vedic Sacrifices in Hinduism." www.hinduwebsite.com/hinduism/vedicsacrifice.asp accessed on 10/31/2016.

28. Rig Veda 10.121.10.

29. It was not a permanent temple, but a residential building that is also used as an office. I was also told that it was part of a movement within Indian Christianity that wants to make Christian faith more "indigenous." Most Christians in India would consider such an attempt a "heresy." There are many Hindu-Christians who make these Prajapati-Christ connections. There are both arguments *for* and *against* it, yet it is part of an "insider movement."

30. Sathapatha Brahmana 10.1.3. 2.

31. The myth of the primordial Adam, found in Gnostic and Essene beliefs. In the Gnostic myth, there was said to have existed in the beginning of creation a spiritual body of light referred to as the primordial Adam (in Gnostic Christianity). This primordial body was broken up by demonic forces into pieces of light, each piece becoming a soul to be born into the world. At the end of time a redeemer was to come to "save" the souls of light, rejoining them into the great spiritual body.

32. Sathapatha Brahmana 11, 1; 8, 2.

33. Sathapatha Brahmana 10.2.2.1–2.

34. Brhadaranykopanisad 3.9.28.4,5.

35. Sathapatha Brahmana 10.1.3.

36. Augilar, H. (1976). *Sacrifice in the Rgveda*. Delhi, Bharatiya Vidya Prakasham. Page 69.

37. Revelation 13:8 NKJV.

38. Bhagavad-Gita IV:7–8.

39. Mark 2:17.

40. Luke 19:10.

41. S Radha Krishnan. *Indian Philosophy* (London: Geprge Allen & Unwin Ltd. 1962.) 108–9.

42. Gandhi, M. K. (1948): *Non Violence in Peace and War*, Volume I, p. 166.

43. Farquhar, page 53, quoted from Satyavrata, God has not left us without Witness.

Chapter 3: The Suffering Savior

1. Yandell, K. and H. Netland (2009). *Buddhism: A Christian Exploration and Appraisal*. Downers Grove, InterVarsity Press. Page 41.

2. Episode 3, season 4, "The Pitch."

3. Keown, D. (2013). *Buddhism: A Very Short Introduction*. Oxford, Oxford University Press. Page 53.

4. Eckel, M. D. *Great World Religions: Buddhism*. The Learning Company.

5. *Skandhas* are constantly shifting components that emerge out of a process called "dependent origination." There are five skandhas:

physical body (*rupa*), sensation (*vedana*), perception (*samjna*), cognition (*sankhara*), and consciousness (*vijnana*).

6. Some scholars are not sure if he was actually a historical figure because most of what we know about him comes from legends and mythologies passed on through oral tradition. We don't have the first written account of his life until Asvaghosha, who compiled *Buddha Charita* (*Life of Buddha*) approximately 600 years after his time, i.e., in the second century CE.

7. Ecclesiastes 1:2.

8. Keown, D. Page 49.

9. Keown, D. Page 57.

10. Ecclesiastes 12:13–14.

11. The fourth Veda of Hinduism, *Atharva Veda*, is considered forbidden because it involves many practices that border black magic only meant to be practiced by trained teachers.

12. The current Dalai Lama is the fourteenth reincarnation of the original Dalai Lama.

13. A popular example, "What is the sound of one hand clapping?"

14. Quoted by Keown, page 121 from Humphreys' "Sixty Years of Buddhism in England," page 80.

15. Muslim emperors considered Buddhists as idol worshippers because there were just as many statues in a Buddhist temple as in a Hindu temple. This is why a religion that is perceived as a harmless nontheistic philosophy is branded an idolatrous religion by the Islamic jihadists.

16. Keown, D. Page 139.

17. Buddhism, for this reason, is often described as the chameleon among world religions. It has the capacity to morph into any shape or form depending on its environment—and indeed has done so at various times and in various locations throughout history.

18. The Message of Buddhism by Bhikkhu Subadhra as quoted in Lodge, B. (1929). *What Is Buddhism?* London, Buddhist Lodge.

19. Eckel, M. D.

20. Gomez, L. *The Land of Bliss: The Paradise of the Buddha of Measureless Light: Sanskrit and Chinese Versions of the Sukhāvatīvyūha.* University of Hawaii Press, 1996.

21. Bodhisattvas are generally identified by six perceptions: generosity (*dana*), morality (*sila*), patience (*ksanti*), courage (virya), meditation (*samadhi*), and wisdom (*prajna*).

22. Keown, D. Page 62.

23. Eckel, M. D.

24. Keown, D. Page 65.

25. Eckel, M. D.

26. Romans 8:28 NKJV.

27. 1506–1552 CE.

28. Reeves, M. (2012). *Delighting in the Trinity: An Introduction to the Christian Faith.* Downers Grove, IVP Academic.

29. 1133–1212 CE.

30. Bary, W. T. D., et al., Eds. (2001). *Sources of Japanese Tradition: Volume 1.* New York, Columbia University Press. Pages 208–9.

31. It was chanted in different languages, but this is an approximate translation I found on the internet. http://terebess.hu/zen/szoto/vows .htm accessed on 12/18/2016.

Chapter 4: The Word Becomes the Lord

1. The Islamic emperors of India unleashed a series of vicious punishments against Sikhs, considering them as heretic Muslims. One of the Sikh

Gurus, Arjan Sing, was boiled in oil and then cut into pieces by the Islamic Mugal emperors of India.

2. Also called *Ek Omkar*, associated with the Hindu Om.

3. Gidoomal, R. and M. Wardell (1996). *Lions, Princesses, Gurus: Reaching Your Sikh Neighbour*. Highland. Page 69.

4. This is a religious rite called "Akhand Path."

5. Guru Nanak made sure that he appointed Gurus from outside his family circle. But after the second Guru, the title became a family heritage. The sixth Guru Har Govind was only nine years old when he assumed the title. The eighth Guru Har Kishan was only five, and he died of smallpox when he turned eight.

6. Guru Granth Sahib 1187–10.

7. Gidoomal, R. and M. Wardell. The text lays out a comparison of the Sat Guru and Jesus.

8. Quoted in Ahmad, S. (1978). *Sikhism and Christian Faith*. Lucknow, Lucknow Publishing House. Page 118.

9. "Sri Guru Granth Sahib." SikhismGuide.org, www.sikhismguide.org /granth.aspx accessed on 11/20/2016.

10. Christ's love for his people is often described as the love of a bridegroom for his bride (Ephesians 5:25; 2 Corinthians 11:2).

11. Please read her story in Scrivens, Mona. (2012) *Jesus According to Sikhism*. Focus Infinity.

12. Singh, N. "Jesus through Sikh Eyes." BBC, October 26, 2009, http://www.bbc.co.uk/religion/religions/sikhism/people/jesus.shtml, accessed on November 11, 2016.

13. Guru Granth Sahib 1136–4.

14. Guru Granth Sahib 943:1.

15. John 1:1.

16. John 1:14.

Chapter 5: The Man Who Became a Sign

1. Trinity, according to Islam, is the worship of three different gods—forbidden in this monotheistic religion.

2. Muhammad's father (Abdulla) died a few days before he was born in 570 CE. His mother (Amina) died when he was around six. His grandfather who cared for Muhammad died when he was eight.

3. Abu Bkr was the father of his last wife, Aisha. Ali was the husband of his daughter Fatimah.

4. John 1:1, 14.

5. Muslims consider the Quran untainted by human influence. However, source criticism points to the fact that the Quran borrowed from a number of preexisting sources such as the Jewish Torah, Christian New Testament, and other Zoroastrian and Arab literature.

6. The first revelation (Sura 96:1–5) came in 610 CE and it continued until Muhammad's death in 632 CE.

7. Jesus is called Isa twenty-five times, Al-Masih eleven times, and Ibn Miriam twenty-three times.

8. Sura 3:49. The childhood stories of Jesus are originally found in apocryphal literature such as Protoevangelium Jacobi (the Infancy Gospel of James) or the Infancy Gospel of Thomas, which church fathers regarded as "too good to be true."

9. Sura 19:29–33.

10. The Arabic word "kalim" does not have the same theological innuendos as the Greek word "logos." Yet, in Islamic thought, it is through His Word that God creates and sustains the universe and reveals His will to the world.

11. Jesus is called Christ/Messiah eleven times (e.g., Sura 5:72).

12. In the history of Islam, many charismatic leaders have presented themselves as messiahs with a divine mandate to establish the rule of God. In Iranian Twelver Shiaism, the twelfth Imam, Muhammad Al Muntazar, is the Al-Mahdi, who will return with Al-Masih (Jesus) in the days of the apocalypse.

13. According to traditional belief, Jesus will get married and live a normal life in the world. Once again, the marriage of Jesus with the church is a theological metaphor used in the Bible, which Muslims interpret as a literal marriage.

14. Hadith Al-Zukruh 43:57–67.

15. Sura 19:22–27.

16. The apostle Paul did a comparison of Jesus and Adam more elaborately in his epistles (1 Corinthians 15:45–49). Paul described Jesus as the second or last Adam, in a sense that Jesus transforms our mortal nature inherited from Adam into His divine nature.

17. Sura 3:59.

18. Muslim apologists argue that another character in the Bible, Melchizedek, is also described as one without father, mother, or descent, and had neither beginning of days nor end of life (Hebrews 7:3). He appears in a brief passage in Genesis 14 where he is described as the king of Salem who met Abraham while returning from a slaughter of the people who captured his nephew Lot. This is again a classic case of theological metaphor. Melchizedek was a type, or a shadow, of the eternal high priest to come. The writer of Hebrews does not say that he actually had no genealogy, but only that it is not recorded in the Scriptures.

19. Genesis 2:4–9; Sura 2:30.

20. Sura 21:91; Sura 66:12.

21. Sura 6:101.

22. More explanation on this term in chapter 7.

23. Sura 4:157.

24. The word is similar to *doekim* (made appear to) from where the heresy of Docetism arises in Gnostic Christianity.

25. The denial of Jesus' crucifixion has its origin in the teachings of apocryphal texts like the Gospel of Barnabas, Acts of John, and others. These documents were widely circulated during the formative years of Islam through the Gnostic Christians, exiled to Arabia by the Byzantine Empire. The Gnostics were charged with their heretic belief in "the unreality of Jesus' suffering." (Cragg, K. (1985). *Jesus and the Muslim: An Exploration.* London, Allen and Unwin. Page 174.) Historians believe that Muhammad "held out an olive branch to Christian Gnostics who denied that Jesus was crucified." (Robinson, N. (1991). *Christ in Islam and Christianity.* Albany, NY, State University of New York Press. Page 110.)

26. Sura 3:55.

27. Josephus, F. (1987). *The Works of Josephus.* Peabody, MA, Hendrickson. 18:63.

28. Tacitus, C. (2004). *The Annals.* Chicago, Hackett. 15:44.

29. There are numerous occasions in which Allah asks Muhammad to confess and repent for his own sins. Sura 40:55/57; 47:19/2; 148:2.

30. Sura 19:19.

31. Abu Huraira (Sahih Muslim, Book 030, Number 5837). This Hadith has been narrated on the authority of Zuhri with the same chain of transmitters (and the words are): "The newborn child is touched by the Satan (when he comes in the world) and he starts crying because of the touch of Satan."

32. Sura 2:67–71.

33. Sura 2:73.

34. Sura 37:107.

35. Zwemer, S. (1912). *The Moslem Christ.* New York, NY, American Tract Society. Page 78. (Originally a quote from TG Huges.)

36. Sura 4:171.

37. Sura 3:49.

38. Sura 3:45.

Chapter 6: The Pierced Messiah

1. (1) The Abrahamic Covenant: God would give the Jewish people the land of Canaan as their inheritance (Genesis 15:18), and through them He would bring ultimate blessing to all nations (Genesis 12:3). (2) The Mosaic Covenant: At Mount Sinai, God gave the Israelites the Law and promised again to give them the land (Exodus 19). (3) The Davidic Covenant: Psalm 89:3–4 and 2 Samuel 7:12–16 record certain promises God made to King David.

2. Luke 4:16.

3. John 10:22–39.

4. Fisher, E. (1993). *Faith without Prejudice: Rebuilding Christian Attitudes Toward Judaism*, Crossroad.

5. Though Jesus appears to have breached the Jewish rites such as Sabbath, in fact, He was only breaking the legalistic codes of Sabbath written by the scribes, not the commandment of Sabbath itself.

6. Flavius Josephus: *Antiquities of the Jews*, book 18, chapter 3, 3. This is one of the most controversial passages in the book, as skeptics think of it as a later insertion by Christians.

7. Itzhaki, Y. (2011). *The Uncovered Head: Jewish Culture*. Newark, University of Delaware Press. Page 100.

8. Rabbi Shapiro, R. M. (2004). *Open Secrets: The Letters of Reb Yerachmiel ben Yisrael*. New York, Monkfish.

9. Genesis 18:1–5.

10. Genesis 32:30.

11. Joshua 5:13–15.

12. Daniel 3:25.

13. God is said to have experienced joy (Isaiah 65:19), grief (Judges 10:16), anger (Deuteronomy 1:37), hatred (Psalm 5:5–6), and love (Jeremiah 31:3), among many other examples.

14. Isaiah 7:14.

15. 2 Samuel 7:12–16.

16. Isaiah 45:1.

17. Encyclopaedia Judaica, Online Version, www.jewishvirtuallibrary.org /jsource/judaica/ejud_0002_0014_0_13744.html, accessed on 11/20/2016.

18. Jeremiah 23:5–6 NKJV; also 33:16.

19. Malachi 4:5–6.

20. Zechariah 13–14.

21. "Who Is Moshiach?—The Basics," www.chabad.org/library/moshiach /article_cdo/aid/1121893/jewish/The-Basics.htm, accessed November 20, 2016.

22. Solomon, N. (2014). *Judaism: A Very Short Introduction*. Oxford, Oxford University Press. Page 136.

23. www.chabad.org/library/moshiach/article_cdo/aid/1121893/jewish /The-Basics.htm accessed 11/20/2016.

24. Shai, C. *The Great Courses: Introduction to Judaism*. The Teaching Company. Guidebook. Page 26.

25. Solomon, N. Page 119.

26. Isaiah 7:14; Micah 5:2.

27. Isaiah 2:2–3; Isaiah 56:6–7; Ezekiel 37:26–27; Micah 4:1–4; Hosea 2:20; Isaiah 2:1–4; Zechariah 3:9; 8:23; 14:9; Isaiah 45:23; Isaiah 66:23; Jeremiah 31:33; Ezekiel 38:23; Psalm 86:9.

28. Zechariah 12:10 NKJV; cf. John 19:37.

29. Many Jewish scholars insist that the Suffering Servant in Isaiah 53 is a figurative description of Israel. But Rabbi Moshe Alsheich, who lived in Palestine in the sixteenth century, wrote: "Our teachers, blessed be their memory, confirmed and unanimously accepted that this chapter speaks about the King Messiah …, who suffers for the iniquities of the children of Israel, and behold, his reward is with him." Rabbi Eliah De Vidas, who lived in Saphed, Israel, at the end of the sixteenth century: "In the same manner that the Messiah suffers for our iniquities which cause him to be bruised, even ours; if anyone wishes that the Messiah should not be bruised for our transgressions, he himself will suffer and be bruised." Quoted from Santala, R. (1992). "How can we be convinced that Jesus is the Messiah?" Bible talks given in Moscow to Messianic Jews.

30. Isaiah 53:2–6.

31. Patai, R. (1979). *The Messiah Text*. Detroit, Wayne State University Press. Page 166.

32. Jeremiah 31:9, 20.

33. Babylonian Talmud Sukkah 52a[8],[9] as quoted by Patai, R. (1979). Page 168.

34. Zechariah 12:10.

35. Deuteronomy 16:1–8.

36. 1 Corinthians 5:7.

37. Luke 22:19; Matthew 26:28.

38. In modern Jewish practice, prayer has taken the place of sacrifice. Jewish people believe that the purposes of sacrifice and prayer are similar: to praise God, to become closer to Him, to express thanksgiving, love, or gratitude.

39. Leviticus 16:15–22.

40. Mishnah Torah, Laws of Teshuvah 1:3. www.chabad.org/library/article _cdo/aid/911888/jewish/Teshuvah-Chapter-One.htm accessed 11/20/2016.

41. Solomon, N. Page 63.

42. Genesis 2:16–17; Ezekiel 18:20; Romans 6:23; Hebrews 10:1–12.

43. Revelation 13:8 NKJV; John 1:29.

44. "Debru Emet: A Recent Statement by Jews on Christianity" (page 44: Judaism II, TLC).

45. Issued on December 3, 2015, it was initially signed by 25 rabbis, but many have added signatures since. The document is available at http://cjcuc.com/site/2015/12/03/orthodox-rabbinic-statement-on-christianity/, accessed on April 24, 2017.

46. *Nostra Aetete.*

47. Based on Moltmann, J. (1993). *Theology of Hope.* Minneapolis, Fortress Press.

48. See Romans 11:25.

49. Quoted from Rabbi Mordechai, K. (2000). *Understanding Judaism: A Basic Guide to Jewish Faith, History, and Practice.* New York, Mesorah. Page 102.

Chapter 7: The Emptied God

1. Frank Viola. Interview with Bono. October 3, 2016, www.patheos.com/blogs/frankviola/bono-on-jesus/, accessed November 20, 2016.

2. Lewis, C. S. (1952). *Mere Christianity.* New York, Harper Collins.

3. Matthew 16:13.

4. Some may argue that this name has prophetic connotations to an eschatological figure we find in the book of Daniel. Daniel 7:13–14 talks about "one like a Son of Man," who is standing for "the saints of the Highest One" (7:18, 21–22) and who will have dominion over all the earth. This might very well be the case, but for an average audience at the time, the son of man only meant an ordinary person.

5. John 8:58.

6. Exodus 3:14.

7. John 14:9.

8. John 10:30.

9. Mark 2:7 NKJV.

10. Virgil, *The Aeneid*. As quoted in Burger, M., Ed. (2015). *Sources for the History of Western Civilization*. Toronto, University of Toronto Press. Page 194.

11. Matthew 16:17.

12. Revelation 1:13–18.

13. Exhortation to the Greeks 1:7:1 (190 CE).

14. The Flesh of Christ 5:6–7 (210 CE).

15. The Fundamental Doctrines 1:0:4 (230 CE).

16. Although the Council of Nicaea was held in 325 CE, the Nicene Creed is believed to have been composed much later in 381 CE.

17. Council of Chalcedon 451 CE.

18. Attributed to Athanasius of Alexandria (296–373 CE).

19. Some would argue that Jesus is a created being based on His title as the "firstborn of all creation" (Colossians 1:15); Revelation 1:5: "the firstborn of the dead"; Colossians 1:18: "the firstborn from the dead"; Romans 8:29: "He would be the firstborn among many brethren." *Firstborn* is a title that shows privilege; it does not always have something to do with the birth order. (Esau's firstborn title is sold to Jacob.) Hebrews 1:2: "In these last days has spoken to us in His Son, whom He appointed heir of all things, through whom also He made the world." In the case of Jesus, the title "firstborn" is mostly a metaphorical usage to describe His power and authority.

20. Lewis, C. S. (1952). *Mere Christianity*. New York, Harper Collins. Page 157.

21. Isaiah 6:1–13.

22. John 12:37–43.

23. John 12:40; Isaiah 6:10; also in 44:18.

24. Exodus 33:18–23.

25. Hebrews 11:26.

26. John 10:33.

27. John 16:30; John 21:17.

28. John 6:64.

29. Matthew 18:20.

30. Matthew 28:18.

31. 1 Timothy 3:16 NKJV; 1 Timothy 1:17; Colossians 1:15; 2 Corinthians 4:4; Hebrews 1:3; Colossians 2:9.

32. Titus 2:13; 1 John 5:20; 2 Peter 1:1.

33. John 14:27.

34. Viola interview with Bono.

35. Matthew 16:25; 2 Corinthians 12:10.

36. Dunstan, S. (1991). "You, Lord, Are Both Lamb and Shepherd." *United Church Hymn Book*, GIA.

Chapter 8: The True Myth

1. Lewis, C. S. (1945). "Christian Apologetics," in *God in the Dock*.

2. Lewis, C. S. (1945). "Myth Becomes Fact," in *God in the Dock*.

3. Lewis, C. S. (1945). "Christian Apologetics," in *God in the Dock*.

4. Richardson, D. (1981). *Eternity in Their Hearts*. Ventura, Regal. Page 56. Richardson has since observed traces of a monotheistic belief system

at the very heart of primitive cultures around the world. Most ancient religions, Richardson argues, promote a belief in an omnipotent "sky god." In China, he is called Shang Ti, the Lord of Heaven, and in Korea, he is Hananim, the Great One. The resemblance of this sky god to the God of the Bible is of particular interest to Richardson. After doing years of fieldwork and data analysis, he concludes: "One of the amazing characteristics of this 'sky god' ... is his propensity to identify himself with the God of Christianity."

5. Holloway, Ronald. (1977) *Beyond the Image: Approaches to the Religious Dimension in the Cinema* (p. 187).

6. Au Hazard Balthazar 1966.

7. "These 'primordial images' or 'archetypes,' as I have called them, belong to the basic stock of the unconscious psyche and cannot be explained as personal acquisitions. Together they make up that psychic stratum which has been called the collective unconscious." Jung, C. (1960) *Collected Works vol. 8*, (1929) *The Significance of Constitution and Heredity in Psychology.* 229–30 (p. 112).

8. 2 Timothy 3:16 NIV.

9. Psalm 19:1.

10. Acts 14:16–17.

11. Romans 2:15.

12. Romans 2:14.

13. Based on *Nostra Aetate* at Vatican 2.

14. Olson, R. (2006). "A Wind That Swirls Everywhere." *Christianity Today*. 50. Page 52.

15. Colossians 1:15.

16. John 6:38.

17. John 14:6.

18. Acts 4:12.

19. According to the Center for the Study of Global Christianity (CSGC) at Gordon-Conwell Theological Seminary, 2011.

20. Mark 9:38–40 and Luke 9:49–50, as we have seen in chapter 1.

21. The fulfillment theology referred to here is a missional theology coming from indigenous mission fields such as the one pioneered by William Miller and John Nicol Farquhar in India. It is different from what is being termed as fulfillment theology, replacement theology, etc., in the Western context in connection with Judaism and Christianity.

22. Titus 2:11.

23. Luke 2:10.

24. Karl Barth, Church Dogmatics I/1 and IV.3.

25. "Religion: Witness to an Ancient Truth." *Time*. April 20, 1962.

26. Egan, H. D. (1986). *Karl Rahner in Dialogue: Conversations and Interviews*. Michigan, Crossroads.

27. Lewis, C. S. (1952). *Mere Christianity*. New York, Harper Collins.

28. Matthew 5:17.

29. Ecclesiastes 3:11.

30. Luke 24:16.

31. Luke 24:31.

32. Isaiah 25:6–8 NIV.

33. Revelation 3:20.

Epilogue

1. Brahadaranyaka Upanishads (I. iii. 28).

2. John 1:9.

BIBLE CREDITS

Unless otherwise noted, all Scripture quotations are taken from the New American Standard Bible®, copyright © 1960, 1995 by The Lockman Foundation. Used by permission. (www.Lockman.org.)

Scripture quotations marked KJV are taken from the King James Version of the Bible. (Public Domain.)

Scripture quotations marked NIV are taken from THE HOLY BIBLE, NEW INTERNATIONAL VERSION®, NIV® Copyright © 1973, 1978, 1984, 2011 by Biblica, Inc.® Used by permission. All rights reserved worldwide.

Scripture quotations marked NKJV are taken from the New King James Version®. Copyright © 1982 by Thomas Nelson. Used by permission. All rights reserved.

See the copyright page for a statement regarding the author's use of religious texts from other faiths.